# Praise for Rudy Wiebe's writing

"What is remarkable about Wiebe's achievement in *The Temptations of Big Bear* and *The Scorched-Wood People*—and now, in *A Discovery of Strangers*—is that he is able to be . . . both Faulkner and Balzac at once. That is, Wiebe can construct scenes of painstaking detail and psychological insight, and combine them or frame them in exciting historical situations. . . ." *–Books in Canada*

"Wiebe continues to do what he does best: capture on a broad canvas many of the epic events in Canadian history . . . a major work of art. Wiebe provides some of the most evocative prose yet about the Canadian North." *–Maclean's*

"The author is a master of descriptive prose. . . . This memorable novel *[A Discovery of Strangers]* will add to the author's reputation as one of Canada's most gifted writers—a peerless delineator of his country's history and soul." *–Canadian Jewish News*

"*Stolen Life* is 'a gift of understanding'—a compelling story infused with hope and spirituality." *–The Financial Post*

"Written with primal intensity, touched with redeeming compassion, Rudy Wiebe has explored our history, our roots and the secrets of our hearts with moral seriousness and great feeling." *–Governor General's Award for Fiction Citation*

# COMHAIRLE CHONTAE ÁTHA CLIATH THEAS
# SOUTH DUBLIN COUNTY LIBRARIES

## BALLYROAN BRANCH LIBRARY
*TO RENEW ANY ITEM  TEL: 494 1900*
*OR ONLINE AT www.southdublinlibraries.ie*

Items should be returned on or before the last date below. Fines, as displayed in the Library, will be charged on overdue items.

# The
# Mad Trapper

Red Deer Press

Copyright © 1980, Jackpine House Ltd.
Revision 2002 Rudy Wiebe
Published in the United States in 2003

5

All rights reserved. No part of this publication may be reproduced, stored in a
retrieval system or transmitted, in any form or by any means, without the prior
written permission of Red Deer Press or, in the case of photocopying or other
reprographic copying, a licence from Access Copyright (Canadian Copyright
Licensing Agency), 1 Yonge Street, Suite 800, Toronto, ON, M5E 1E5, fax (416)
868-1621.

Published by Red Deer Press
195 Allstate Parkway, Markham
ON, L3R 4T8
www.reddeerpress.com

Credits
Cover design by Daniel Blais
Text design by Dennis Johnson, assisted by Daniel Krut
Map by Laura Golins
Printed and bound in Canada

We acknowledge with thanks the Canada Council for the Arts, and the Ontario
Arts Council for their support of our publishing program. We acknowledge the
financial support of the Government of Canada through the Canada Book Fund
(CBF) for our publishing activities.

Canada Council    Conseil des Arts          ONTARIO ARTS COUNCIL
for the Arts      du Canada                 CONSEIL DES ARTS DE L'ONTARIO

Library and Archives Canada Cataloguing in Publication
Wiebe, Rudy, 1934–
The mad trapper / Rudy Wiebe.
(Northern lights young novels)
ISBN 0-88995-268-X
I. Johnson, Albert, d. 1932 – Fiction. I. Title. II. Series.
PS8545.138M33 2002      C813'.54      C2002-904717-X
PR9199.3.W47M3 2002

Photo credits

Cover photo courtesy of Glenbow Museum
Page 16, Glenbow Archives NA-1685-1
Page 19, Glenbow Archives NA-1258-109
Page 27, Glenbow Archives NA-1631-1
Page 66, Glenbow Archives NA-3844-90
Page 74, Glenbow Archives NA-1258-103
Page 82, Glenbow Archives NA-1685-3
Page 92, Glenbow Archives NA-1258-114
Page 109, Lazarus Sittichinli in 1926, courtesy I.S. MacLaren, from
The Ladies, the Gwich'in, and the Rat (1998). Photo by Clara Coltman Rogers
(late Lady Vyvyan); collection of Edward Zealley.
Page 114, Glenbow Archives NA-3622-16
Page 144, Glenbow Archives NA-1258-115
Page 178, Glenbow Archives NA-1258-117
Page 184, Glenbow Archives NA-1258-119
Page 188, City of Edmonton Archives EA-27-3

# Contents

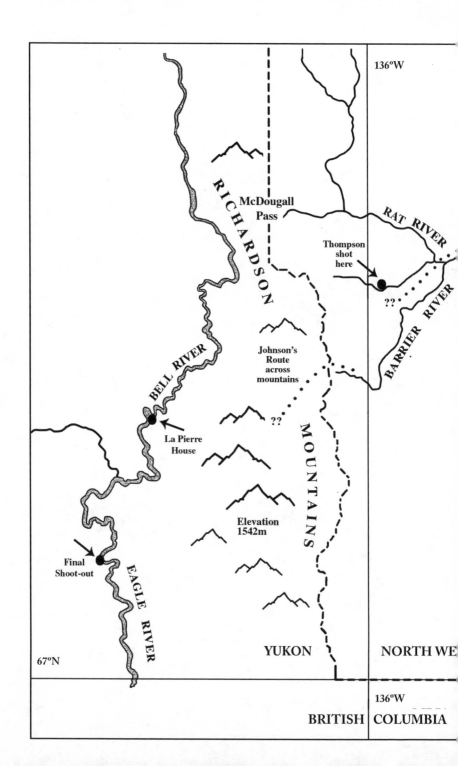

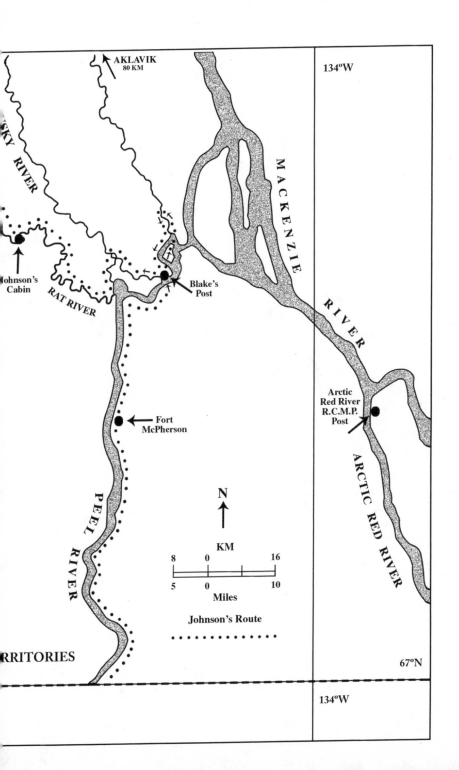

*Part One*

# Stranger

# 1

THE AUTUMN SUN was almost gone behind the Richardson Mountains. Its last light flamed against an underbelly of cloud, polished the water of the Peel River into uneasy boils of glistening black and vivid, almost bloody, red. Distant sounds drifted by: geese flying south, water lapping against rocks, but over all lay the immense Arctic silence of the coming winter.

A spot of blackness appeared on the edge of a red gleam that cut across the river. Slowly the spot grew larger, lengthened into the light so slowly that it seemed to be standing still in the gleaming water without a ripple or a wave to reveal its movement. Gradually the shape emerged: in the middle of the huge empty river was a man.

Squatting on a three-log raft. A long pole lay across his legs folded in front of him and his body and head were bent forward in exhaustion, perhaps sleep; but his arms were braced so wide and solidly on his knees that he held himself erect, balanced on the narrow raft by sheer determination. While the relentless will of the current carried him steadily north.

# 2

AT FORT MCPHERSON, a hundred miles north of the Arctic Circle, William Douglas was giving his annual trappers' dance. There wasn't much dancing space in his trading post, not even when they pushed the three long counters back tight against the wall shelves, but with the fiddlers up on the main counter with him while he called the squares, the dancers had some room to swing their partners. In any case, tomorrow most of them would leave for their winter trap lines scattered across the numberless lakes and channels of the Mackenzie River Delta and into the foothills of the Richardson Mountains; they might not see another person all winter so a bit of crowding now, rubbing together was fine, just fine.

"Swing that girl, the girl so sweet," Douglas called bobbing on the counter in his dress-plaid kilt, "swing that girl with the two left feet."

The people of Fort McPherson whirled to the foot-stomping shrill of the fiddles. They spun under the noses of their friends who crowded up against the counters and spilled out through the open door into the evening darkness. From where the musicians sat above them they looked like turning patches of colour, bright checked shirts and blouses, the red and purple shawls of the women flung back from their shining black hair. Gwich'in Dene and Metis and Inuit men and women, white men of every shade and accent were caught in the boisterous dance; the cans on the shelves bounced, the hanging mantle lamps swung to the drum of their moccasined feet.

"Time to eat!" bellowed a blond giant whose head stuck out above the crowd. In either big hand he held high a cream-decorated chocolate pie, waving them like round semaphores at Douglas. "Eat! Hey, Bill, I've gotta EAT before I can dance some more!"

The music was drowned for a moment in laughter, shouting.

"Go on, Knut, when could you ever dance?"

"You're nothing but gut!"

"Get your big meathooks outa them pies!"

A tall Royal Canadian Mounted Police corporal in scarlet dress uniform twirled in the dance to come up nose to long nose against the blond trapper. The policeman laughed aloud at the giant standing there suddenly startled, hands helplessly up balancing pies, but then he was immediately spun away by the bare arm of his Dene partner.

"Do the dance you did before, and pop that couple under," called Douglas, oblivious to the waving pies and the huge mouth whose roar he could no longer hear. The entire building shook to the thud-slide-thud of the furious dance.

Edgar "Spike" Millen, RCMP officer

# 3

IN THE LAST SUNLIGHT darting off the muddy river, the man still sat bent forward on his narrow raft. He could have been drifting that way for days, even weeks or months. Perhaps he had found the Peel River somewhere near its source four hundred miles away in the craggy Ogilvie Mountains of the Yukon and had built his raft and settled himself like this, motionless but balanced to the endless unrolling of the river while it carried him east between the sharp slab teeth of those mountains and then north through the thousand-foot canyons of the Peel Plateau and past islands and over the braided channels of gravel bars to this wide, lake-like movement paralleling the Richardson Mountains. He sat so easily, so much at one with the give of the river that he could have been floating all summer and now through the brief fall and on until winter crushed its surface together in jagged ice.

But suddenly the man moved. His head lifted a little, as if he were listening. Though he might merely have been looking at the small pack and bedroll lying in front of him, at the Savage 30-30 rifle, featherweight model, propped across it so that he had only to shift his right hand slightly to slip it through the trigger guard.

The river chuckled between the logs.

In one smooth motion the man stood up. One instant he was sitting, bent forward, and the next he was on his feet with the pole in his hands so easily the raft gave no ripple in the golden water. The man was of medium height and barrel chested; half of his face was caught by the red of the vanishing sun, which outlined the weathered scars, the stubbled whiskers and broken-peaked cap. He stared forward, intent on the high right bank of the river valley far ahead.

Tiny lights winked there. Small humps of buildings stood against the bristle of spruce and the lighter darkness of the north-eastern sky.

And there were sounds too. He could hear them now as he concentrated on listening. He could not tell what they were, but sounds came to him, carried and then taken away by the sharp evening air.

After a moment he straightened up. Heavily, as if lifting a burden. He slipped the long pole into the river. Down, down, and then he touched the rocky bottom twelve feet below. He leaned, pushed hard, and the raft started away at an angle, leaving a line with a whorl beside it where he drew up his pole. He leaned down over his pack and rifle and pushed again, and again, in long powerful strokes. And gradually the man's craggy face hardened into a fixed, solid grimace as the line in the gleaming water lengthened towards the far right shore.

# 4

"GO ON WITH YOU, KNUT," the tall police corporal was laughing open mouthed, "it'd be no contest, you and me!"

The crowd turned from clapping the musicians, who were reaching for well-earned drinks, to the two tall men facing each other. The blond trapper, Knut Lang, swished the chocolate pies together past the policeman's lean face and appealed to everyone in the store.

"You hear that?" he roared in his thick Norwegian accent, "I challenge him fair and square, but he's scared. Spike Millen's scared!"

The Dene women giggled, the men hooted with laughter at such absurdity. A man with a gaunt weathered face, whose worn overalls and bleached shirt were out of place among the bright flannels and tanned caribou hide, could not take his eyes off the sweet pie swinging by so close in front of him. His hand moved out, his finger searched blindly for that soft twirled cream.

"I'm scared all right," shouted Millen, "of your big mouth!"

"Hey!" Lang jerked the pie aside, "No dirty fingers, eh?" and the weathered farmer had to turn away, swallowing, while everyone laughed. "You all heard me, fair and square, I challenge Spike."

Only one man was not laughing. Constable Alfred King stood in immaculate red dress uniform near the door and kept his eye on everyone. He saw, with undisguised distaste, that his superior danced with any woman and bantered with any man. King had been a policeman in the Arctic almost as long as Millen, five years, and several times during the year he had been stationed at Fort McPherson he had mentioned what he thought was the proper, dignified behaviour that Royal Canadian Mounted Police officers should display. Corporal Millen listened to him, all right, but always argued back quite agreeably. "If you

K. H. "Knut" Lang, Trapper

can't have dignity while being friendly too, what the world good are you as a policeman?" was the gist of his argument. And King knew he was right; of course, a policeman was a human being, but to get into such silly mix-ups like shouting arguments, contests—no.

"We all know why you won't eat that pie," a stocky trapper in a moose-hide jacket yelled at Millen, grinning hugely. "You baked it, that's why you're scared!"

That was the trouble, thought King as the laughter rolled around him. Edgar Millen was a good police officer, better than any he had ever worked under, but he did such silly things. He had the reputation of being the best dancer and pie baker down the two thousand miles of Mackenzie River and he had to prove both at every party. No wonder everyone just called him by his nickname, "Spike"—tall and lean with shoulders like a weight lifter—even "Ed" would have been more respectful. The RCMP had policed the enormous Canadian Arctic since the Yukon gold rush in 1898, there was a certain formal distance that the law should maintain. It must, King thought.

A wiry Metis trapper, Noel Verville, pulled out a handful of crumpled bills, pondered them a moment and selected two. "Ten dollars on Spike," he said heavily, challenging the men with his eyes, his raised hand. "Three to one on Spike."

"You bet on Spike, Noel, so he'll remember next time you're drunk!"

Verville barely grinned, shaking his money above heads in the roaring crowd; many of them had been in the brawl with him in September when Millen had arrested and thrown them all into jail with complete impartiality.

"You ever help me in a fight, Sid, I pay your fine," he yelled. "Three to one, huh?"

"Twenty on Knut Lang," said the man in the moose-hide jacket. "Two to one, at twenty?"

"My god," said the man in worn overalls, "if I had money like that, I'da stayed on my farm in Saskatchewan."

Millen glanced swiftly at the man, then to Lang's long, bony face grinning at him like a cat across the pies. Fur prices were very good— apparently the rich could afford them even during a depression—and the big Norwegian would make a small fortune again; but this winter of 1931–32 was going to be very hard on these southern men who left their ruined farms to try and make a little winter money trapping rats on the delta. There had been two of them at Fort McPherson last year, this year there were more. It was hard to convince them the high Arctic wasn't like northern Saskatchewan: even if a man knew how to trap, there was still the long heavy weather and the loneliness. And in December and January the weeks with barely an hour of light: the long darkness as the native Peoples called it. But this worn farmer . . . Millen glanced at him again and in that instant made up his mind. He clapped the man on his bony shoulder.

"You have to have confidence in yourself," he said quietly, then looked into Lang's blue eyes. "Okay Knut," he shouted, "you're on!"

The crowd burst into cheering; hands clutching money waved everywhere, the racket in the small room rattled the windows. Constable King grimaced; Millen could never resist a challenge and that crafty devil Lang knew it. There were more dark men pushing in from outside, drawn by the yells of betting, and King backed between them, out into the cold evening air. Tomorrow, he thought, more than a few wives would be cursing their men when the dollars they thought they had were missing. Well, a few might have more than they had expected—if they bet lucky. Lang's mouth was certainly bigger.

King turned and stood on the narrow step of Douglas's trading post. He could look west down the long dark valley towards the wide band of the river still bright in the sunset, the low, saw-toothed outline of distant mountains beyond. The Dene in for trading were camped on the flats along the river: he could see the sprawl of greyish tents and the campfires blinking between them, the black shapes of overturned canoes and of people moving there, of the sled dogs sitting at the ends of their chains and waiting all summer for snow so they could again be set free into harness and drudgery. Momentarily the shout of betting ceased behind him—they must have started to stuff themselves—from a tent below he heard a baby cry. And quickly the sound was gone, like a breast thrust into an open mouth.

A spot on the bright river caught King's eye and he squinted, trying to see. He had to stare southwest directly into the last light falling behind the Richardson Mountains, and red spots danced before his eyes. Impossible light. It had seemed too tall, somehow, to be a canoe. What he had seen of it.

The cheering intensified behind him and he tried to peer into the store. That, too, was impossible; men were jammed there, waving their money high and yelling "Knut!" "Spike!" while craning to see what was happening. Three Dene children raced past him, circling the trading post and shrieking with such excitement that suddenly a dog on the slope below began to howl. Then another and another. An Arctic settlement night, King thought; he was used to it, the usual small noises of man and beast that vanished like nothing into enormous stillness.

And at the centre of the crowd Edgar "Spike" Millen and Knut Lang were eating chocolate pie. With their hands clasped behind them and mouths agape, they bent to the edge of the counter where their assistants nudged the pies forward as fast as they could work their faces into them. The crowd whistled, cheered, jumped with excitement around them, thrust fists of money so close that three burly men had to keep pushing them back to give the labouring champions eating space. Lang ate voraciously. He urged his assistant, with nods of his shaggy head, to shove the pie forward faster even though half of it seemed smeared over his face and neck, and gobs of cream sprayed from his gesturing head. Millen's cooperation with his assistant seemed better. His pie was moving ahead more cleanly, but his planned, deliberate eating gradually broke down as the outer crust came closer: he was ear-to-ear chocolate, an immense brown grin smeared across his face as bits of crust flew, but his uniform was still immaculate.

"Eat, Knut, eat, you bastard!" roared the man in the moose-hide jacket.

The weathered farmer, hunched between two yelling Metis trappers, did not make a sound. He was rigid, staring at Millen while clutching a worn twenty-dollar bill.

Lang was ahead. His backers began their roar of triumph as the last glob of chocolate and crust lurched into his gaping maw, but then his assistant roared in pain, "My thumb, god my thumb!" and Lang's mouth boiled out pie as the assistant jerked back, shaking his hand and dancing on the counter in agony. At that moment Millen's arm went up: his pie was all in his mouth and Lang was using his own hands to stuff the last crust back into his: a clear foul, a clear victory.

"Hurrah for Spike Millen!" bellowed Noel Verville, waving money, and all the Millen backers—everyone in the room, it now seemed— roared into cheers.

"We had him, Knut," the assistant said blackly, still massaging his thumb, "we had him till you . . ."

Lang's mouth and throat were still too full; all he could do was shake his huge body, but clearly he would have a lot to say in a minute. "Always going for the meat, you bastard," the man in the moose-hide jacket said. "It was a pie contest."

The farmer stared at two new twenty-dollar bills now lying in his hand on top of his worn twenty.

"Son of a—" he looked at Millen in amazement. "This woulda fed all my kids in Saskatchewan three months."

"Send it to them . . . fast," Millen was still gulping for breath. "When it comes that . . . quick it can go just . . . like that. Hey, Knut," he turned, gasping in the big man's blotched face, "I was wrong. Your mouth isn't so big."

"Ha no?" Lang roared, triumphant anyway. "But I ate one good pie, the whole one myself!"

"You smart son of a gun," Millen chuckled into the laughter from the crowd, and punched the trapper in the shoulder. "Whew, I'm not so sure." He was rubbing his stomach ruefully.

The crowd noise broke into talk again. Outside the dogs barked furiously, clearly with purpose. Millen glanced about: King was not in the store so let him handle that if it needed handling. He wheeled to Douglas and the musicians on the counter.

"Enough of this . . . eating!" he shouted over heads. "Mr. Douglas, we need dancing music, music!"

"Of course, Corporal Millen, at your command, sir, at your command," Douglas answered with exaggerated politeness. "Honour your partners for the Scottish reel!"

Millen found himself facing an older Dene woman, her shape rounded soft by shawl and long dress to her moccasined feet. He reached for her hand.

"May I have the pleasure?"

The woman looked up at him quickly and her face crumpled; she turned away laughing high, merrily. Around her the other women giggled and hooted, nudging each other. He put his hand up to his face, his fingers slipped and then he became aware of more and more chocolate. Quickly he reached for the woman's smooth worn hand again as the fiddlers picked up the rhythm Douglas was tapping on the counter with his foot.

"Would you care to dance, madam," Millen bowed gravely, "with a chocolate Mountie?"

And, still laughing, she did.

# 5

William Nerysoo was placing two split logs on the campfire in front of his tent when the sound of the dogs changed. He looked through the sparks and flames at his young wife Celeste nursing their baby in the firelight. Her dark face glowed as she smiled at him.

"Must be somebody coming," he said, gesturing to the dogs growling all around the camp. "On the river."

"Maybe somebody else with money to gamble," Celeste said, listening to the cheers from the trading post on the bank above them. She was happy with her big man across the fire from her, that he hadn't gone up for the betting.

Her tiny boy stopped nursing and she looked down at him, laughing at his milk-stained mouth. Then she lifted him across her shoulder and patted him gently as he burbled.

Nerysoo stood up. He came around the fire and bent down, brushed his fingers between her full breasts heavy against her opened shirt.

"Better put that away," he said. "It's probably a man."

Celeste's soft laughter followed his as he walked down the slope to the river. He moved between tents and dogs with the smooth easy grace of a man who has carried himself by his own strength wherever he has needed to travelled.

A cluster of Gwich'in Dene men were already on the river's edge. They were watching the small raft come towards them, the shape on it poling slant and straight despite the powerful current. Against the light they could just see the movement, bending long, rhythmically.

"Looks like another poor white bugger," one man said as Nerysoo came up.

"Yeah," said another. "Wonder how far he floated on that."

"Just about like balancing on one log," the first said.

"He sure never come through the canyon rapids like that," the second said.

"Not unless he has gills," Nerysoo said, and they all laughed quietly.

"Maybe it has," another Dene said thoughtfully, and they all laughed again at the "it," though somewhat uneasily now. The narrow balance of the raft, so tall out of the water and coming like an arrow at them did seem incredible, almost as if the shape were sliding on the glazed river, walking on it. But the dogs chained where the raft was heading in to shore were going berserk; it was no spirit, no, clearly it must be a man. The men shifted their feet nervously on the gravel.

"That might be Karl Erickson's cousin," Nerysoo offered matter-of-factly. When the old people told stories around the campfires of meeting a *nana'?ih* spirit in the long darkness, he always said that could be so, but he'd never met one, not yet.

The raft slid onto mud and stopped. The shape straightened up into a stocky man, up as if he were looking at them, then around at the scattered white tents in the darkness of the slope behind them and up to the blazing windows of the trading post where music scraped furiously to the steady thud of feet. Finally as if becoming aware of an annoyance, the man swung his long pole at the dogs furiously baying at him. He knocked one on the head, another on the flank and they yelped aside to the length of their chains. He dropped the pole across the raft and then bent to pick up his rifle before he stepped on shore.

The Dene men could now see in the dull glow off the river that he was a white man, so they said nothing. But the stranger said nothing either, not so much as one word of casual greeting. After studying the men a moment he picked the small pack and bedroll off the raft with his left hand, without quite turning his back on them, and stepped across the mud bar to the gravel.

"Shut up you dogs," Nerysoo said, clearing a path between them with his feet. Several other men did the same, kicking the animals into yelping silence.

The man shouldered into his pack, his rifle hanging free and easy in his right hand. As he came forward there was the sound of footsteps on the slope behind them.

"Hello," Nerysoo said to the man in English.

Water chuckled between the logs of the raft.

The stranger said nothing. It seemed almost as if he had timed his arrival for the footsteps to come down the slope just then for suddenly there was Constable Alfred King. Alert and ready as always. The Dene stood silent; several of them shuffled aside a little.

King studied the tiny raft a moment, then the man. His face was hidden in the darkness under his cap's peak . . . with no outfit like that, where in the world would he have come from? To reach the sources of the Peel River you had to climb stone mountain ranges. One rifle and one knapsack? Puzzled, King laughed a little and tried for a joke.

"Say," he said, "that's a awful slow way of getting here!"

But nobody laughed. Like the jokes of all humourless men, it, was worse than no comment at all and King knew it by the restless shuffles. The man was staring at him expressionlessly, the rifle moving slightly in his hand.

"Well..." King looked uncomfortably down at the raft again, and suddenly a thought struck him, "Hey, are you Albert Johnson?" He glanced around at the Dene, "Karl Erickson was in here waiting for his cousin Johnson, wasn't he?"

"Yeah," Nerysoo said slowly. "Erickson was, all fall. Waiting."

The man was looking intently from Nerysoo to King. It was clear he did not like the policeman's pushy attempt at camaraderie, but at the same time he was trying to understand something that might be of importance to him; collecting information quickly.

There was a pause. The man looked at Nerysoo suddenly. The policeman was there, huge in his ornate scarlet clothes, but obviously the man was not going to talk to him; not if he could help it.

"Where'd he go?" he asked. "Erickson?"

"North and west," Nerysoo gestured. "Over the mountains maybe."

"It was getting too late to lay out a trap line," King cut in loudly, "he couldn't wait any more. What's your name?"

The man stared at him. Even in the darkness they could all see his face tightening with anger.

"Well?" King demanded. He was used to the Dene looking at the ground, glancing off into the distance. This angry glare from under the darkness of the peaked cap pushed him, he knew it, into too much loudness. "Are you Albert Johnson?"

Alfred W. King, RCMP officer

The stranger deliberately ignored the policeman and stared at William Nerysoo now, almost as if he would read his answer on that broad, strong Dene face.

"Yeah," he said abruptly, the word clipped and furious.

"Okay," King said ignoring the tone, relieved. "Okay, why don't you say so? You'll have a rough time finding your cousin now. He's somewhere up in that wilderness and canyons out west laying out a trap line, and in two weeks the river'll be jammed with ice so—" King caught himself; he was talking too much. Good police technique was to let the other person do the talking, but this man . . . his voice sounded like he hadn't spoken in a month. And to come down the rough Peel River into the Arctic with such an outfit, like a drifting beggar, well.

"Come on up to the store," he said as kindly as he could, turning to go. "At least there's plenty of free food here tonight. A party, come on and eat."

King went, and so he did not see Johnson glaring after him, his whole body held rigid in a fierce, suppressed fury. But Nerysoo saw, and the other Dene men too. Rage had suddenly stiffened the stranger like sweat bursting out of every pore, and they moved uneasily on the gravel. Nerysoo felt a twinge of apprehension, and then he noticed the raft again. The current had pulled it around, was tugging at it. He said, "The river will take it."

Johnson wheeled, stepped down and with a fierce, quick violence kicked at the raft with his heavy boots. Again and again, pounding until it bobbed free and then he lurched into the muddy water and kicked it again so that it wobbled well out from shore, finding the current.

The Dene watched in silent amazement.

Johnson swung around, shrugged his small pack and bedroll squarely onto his shoulders, and came out of the water and up the bank. His sharp peaked face, his short broad body coiled and swinging that rifle like a whip, lashing, moved between the Dene as if they were not there. He strode away, north along the mud and gravel edge of the river, away from both the tents and the trading post still throbbing with dance music.

"Whu-uh!" grunted one man, shaking his head.

"Wouldn't want to meet that," said another, "alone in the bush."

"Yeah," said William Nerysoo, watching the figure grow smaller," . . . yeah."

# 6

In the store the dancing was over and the eating well begun. Children chased each other between the adults, gobbling jam-smeared bannock, screaming when they were caught or pummelled. The men and women stood in clusters, drinking tea black as tar, their happy faces glistening in the yellow light of the hissing mantle lamps.

"You know," the weathered fanner said, his mouth full of dried apricots, "the last wheat I had went three bushel to the acre. Three bushel!"

"You don't buy much of nothing with that," Knut Lang was packing his pipe carefully.

"Yeah, so what good's a tractor? Last spring there was so much dust in the wind my McCormack-Deering got covered right up, I don't even know exactly where it is."

"Huh?" Noel Verville said. "You don't know where it is?"

"Wind," said the farmer, "drifting the topsoil like snow, sand drift higher'n this room. Buried my tractor right outta sight."

Lang swore incredulously in Norwegian.

"Wind, hell," the farmer bragged in the circle of astonished faces, "my neighbour once tried to walk across his yard when the wind was blasting sand like that and when he got to the barn he wasn't wearing no pants. Sanded clean off him."

Spike Millen had another pie in his hand, an apple pie this time. Turning it a little on his finger tips, he was explaining in slow, careful English to a small group of very attentive, though mystified Gwich'in Dene women.

"The trick with pie crust is to make it with pig lard. Bear grease is no good, it's got to be lard."

"What's that, 'pig'?" an older woman said.

"It's a fat beast with a square nose and about so high—" Millen stopped, sensing their laughter about to burst from their grinning faces. "Annie," he threatened the questioner, "you are making fun of me again."

The women, all except Annie, were giggling behind their hands.

"That's okay," said Annie. "You ever make pie on a open fire?"

Millen gestured in mock despair as their merriment rolled over him, uproariously. He surrendered, completely, thrust the apple pie into Annie's quick hands and turned in pretended flight while their laughter followed him. And there was King, coming through the crowd towards him. News on his face.

"We've got another one on our hands," King said morosely, coming up.

Millen broke a piece of bannock from the stack on the counter beside him.

"Another what?"

"Displaced farmer. That cousin Karl Erickson was waiting for just floated in on a three-log raft and nothing for a outfit, absolutely nothing."

Millen dipped his bannock in a tin of strawberry jam a small boy offered him.

"Was Erickson still expecting him to come?" he asked. "He's gone."

But King was not listening. His busy eyes were scanning the crowd, and they had found William Nerysoo moving sideways through the people towards the food table.

"That farmer coming to eat?" King asked as Nerysoo came up.

"Don't know," Nerysoo said. "He just kicked his raft into the river and walked off."

"He say anything about trying to find Erickson?" King insisted.

"He said nothing," Nerysoo said, his mouth full of jam. "He just walked away, down river."

"I guess that means he's staying," Millen grinned.

Nerysoo laughed. "Anyways, I don't think he's a farmer."

"What do you mean?" King asked.

"Not the way that rifle fits his hand."

King thoughtfully watched Nerysoo's broad back thread its way through the crowd and disappear.

"I think," he said slowly, "I'll just go ask Johnson a few questions."

Millen glanced up quickly, put out his hand to stop him turning. "No," he said. "He'll want to sleep, travelling this late."

"All he had for outfit Spike, was that one little knapsack and his—"

"Leave him alone," Millen said quietly, and turned.

He caught the arm of a tiny girl flying past, swung her up above everyone into the air and as her high happy screams drew the crowd's attention, he pushed his way through to the main counter.

"Hear ye, hear ye!" he shouted, twirling the small body in one hand like a banner above his head. A fiddler tapped hard and clear on his violin. Millen spun the wriggling, shrieking girl down to the floor and thrust his last bit of jam and bannock at her.

"Eat that and get to bed!" he glowered down in mock fierceness. She gasped, laughing open mouthed, and snatched the food.

"Listen," Millen raised his head and told all the people, their faces so good and familiar to him, "some of you want to trade tomorrow before you leave for your trap lines. So this better be the last dance. I wish you good health, good trapping, good hunting. If you have problems, anything, get a message to us. Constable King and I are here to help. And we'll try to make two patrols all around this winter, you can count on us, one right after Christmas and one beginning of March. So, we'll see you all in your camps. And when you get tired of the cold and the snow, remember: down south in Edmonton and Toronto they've got soup lines from here to the river. Okay, one more good dance, everybody!"

The fiddlers sawed into a square dance as the crowd cheered. Douglas clambered up on the counter, kilts flying.

"Honour your partners," he called. "Give right hands to partners, left hands to opposites, balance four in line!"

# 7

THE STRANGER who had admitted he was Albert Johnson squatted before a tiny fire of smokeless dry sticks. His knapsack was laid open to an orderly arrangement of his few supplies on his left, his rifle lay along his right leg. A tent, just large enough to contain his opened bedroll, stood behind him.

He was camped high on a height of land, bare except for large scattered rocks such as he had used to weigh down the corners of his tent. There was no wind; a steely, clear night hardening down into cold under moon and stars. Far on his left were humped the few buildings of Fort McPherson with their lit windows and the campfires of the trapper camp blazing up and dying quickly, the long Anglican church with its short steeple. In front of him stretched the wide pale river, straight south like a livid highway in the direction from which it had brought him, and curving past him to the right towards the Mackenzie River and its immense tangled delta that pushed its way in countless intersections and channels north into the always ice-covered Arctic Ocean. By moving his head slightly he could see in any direction: he could not be approached except over open ground. Occasionally he glanced up and around as if contemplating the rocky barrenness all about him. The thin distant sounds of high laughter, fiddles, the howling of a dog from Fort McPherson did not move his head.

The fire snapped, flamed up and died a little against the black tea tin sitting in its nest of coals. On a movement of air like breathing came the far call of a child, came and vanished as quickly.

The man leaned forward, with a stick hooked the tea tin out and set it on the ground beside his rifle. Without taking his eyes from the fire he reached to an exact spot in his knapsack for a small package of sugar. It was almost empty. He poured it leisurely, almost granule by white granule into the steaming tea and then put the empty sack back in its place. He stirred the tea with the stick and, after a moment, drank. Sipping, the tin very hot to his lips but obviously welcome to his hard hands.

After a time he reached to another corner of the knapsack and his left hand found a small, round, red and blue box. Dodds Kidney Pills. He twisted the lid off: there were only two tiny pills left. He looked down at them, his eyes fixed as if he were not seeing anything, his face thoughtful and concentrated beyond whatever he held in his hand. His mouth opened, as if words were actually shaping themselves there.

"Never smile at a woman," he murmured aloud, not actually talking nor singing either but making a sound somewhere between the two. "Call no man your friend. If you trust . . ."

His voice trailed away into silence. He dropped the two pills into his mouth, lifted the tea tin, and washed them down.

Wind came at him then on the open hill. Smelling of distance, glaciers, of mountains like teeth. The tent knocked behind him, the sting of north and coming snow and winter brushed him through his autumn jacket. He was staring at the small round box in his hands, the red and white words: Dodds . . . Dodds . . . a name, a name, everything had to have a name. Everybody. Abruptly he placed it on the coals.

The tiny points of fire licked around the cardboard and suddenly it burst, curled up black into flaming scarlet. The man's face remained hard, clenched and motionless as he stared at the words on the small box burning into light.

# 8

IN THE EARLY GREY MORNING, the people at Fort McPherson were breaking camp. Men melted tar in small cans over fires while cutting canvas to patch their canoes; women packed utensils, cans, and sacks of flour and sugar in waterproof bags. Little girls fed babies propped upright in their cradleboards while boys held dogs so their mothers could lash packs tight onto their backs. Snow was late this year, and everything would have to be moved by canoe or on foot.

Knut Lang was trying to bargain William Nerysoo out of two half-grown pups tumbling over each other and their own big feet.

"Come on, Bill," Lang argued. "You've got lots of dogs. I need them right now if I'm gonna train them."

"I'll have to ask my woman," Nerysoo said, and Lang roared with laughter. "I will," the Dene insisted. "She'll have to pull this winter if I don't have enough dogs."

Lang looked at Celeste, bent in a slender arc of tanned, fringed moose hide over their baby. He swallowed, grinning at Nerysoo, not ashamed of the envy that showed on his face.

"Then don't work so hard," he chuckled a little. "You won't have so many furs to haul."

"It's tough you know," grinned Nerysoo, "keeping a beautiful woman."

Further down the village, Corporal Edgar Millen leaned against the cemetery fence in front of the Anglican church, deep in talk with the weathered farmer who had won his bet the night before. Millen was not in dress scarlet now but in serviceable winter drab; his thin, handsome face still showed the party in a few streaks of dried chocolate a hasty morning shave had missed. The farmer grimly studied the wooden grave markers while Millen talked as he always did: as much with his hands as with his mouth.

"I don't know how big a territory King and I have to patrol, not in miles. Hell, all we have to know is how long it takes. If we had a plane like Lindbergh flew through here last summer we could probably get all around it in two days."

"Two days, flying?" The farmer was staggered.

"A patrol by sled is about a month, give or take a little weather, and by canoe it's longer."

"Then why . . . ?" the man gestured, and Millen laughed aloud.

"If we don't come around you probably won't see a thing that moves for seven months, except maybe a fox. You got any idea how empty this country is? And deadly, six weeks without sun and forty-five, fifty below?"

"It gets that cold in Saskatchewan."

"Once every two years, and not in the dark. Look, I grew up in Edmonton, that's California compared to this."

The farmer looked at him with morose apprehension. "Then how does anybody live up here?" he said at last.

"Easy," Millen grinned, "you live here as good as anywhere, but you've got to know how. And once or twice a winter a friendly cop drops in to warm up and drink a cup of tea."

"Sounds more like suicide," the farmer said heavily.

"Hell no!" Millen laughed. "But you've sure got to know how, so watch the Dene Indians. They've lived here just fine for five thousand years."

Inside the trading post Douglas and his assistant had rearranged the counters for business. A small group of Metis and white trappers lounged in the open centre, waiting their turn, watching Douglas flip a few more beads on his abacus and glance up as his assistant added five boxes of shotgun shells to the huge pile of supplies already heaped up. Clearly the trader was in a quandary.

"And fifty pounds of sugar," Albert Johnson said. He stood slightly stooped, one hand on the counter, his 30-30 rifle hanging butt up over his left shoulder.

Douglas looked at the total on the abacus, then at the supplies Johnson had already ordered. Two hundred-pound sacks of flour and one of rice, four smaller sacks of tea, slabs of bacon, shirts, pants, socks, rolls of stove-pipe, a single-shot Iver-Johnson shotgun, a .22 Winchester,

twenty boxes of 30-30 bullets . . . as if he were going to arm an army.
Douglas gestured to his assistant. Fifty pounds of sugar was about right,
but—

"Those pills," Johnson interrupted his thought. "Dodds."

Douglas turned, took the opened carton off the shelf behind him.
One of a dozen boxes had been sold.

"One or two boxes?"

"All of them."

Douglas looked up. The other trappers were a dark silent circle
against the brightness of the store windows, watching intently.

"There's fifty pills in each box," Douglas said, "and those eleven
boxes there's—"

He stopped. Johnson was glaring at him, his grey eyes furious and
hard like chipped iron. The trader placed the carton on the counter,
flipped the abacus as his assistant heaved the sack of sugar onto the
counter.

"Listen, Mr. Johnson," Douglas said not looking at the man, ignoring the anger he felt clenched across the counter from him, "no one
knows you here, now I know you need an outfit for winter but I can't
give you this much credit. You have—"

"How much?" Johnson gestured stiffly. Almost as if he held the rifle
in his hand, Douglas thought with a jolt. He looked down at the abacus quickly.

"Seven hundred forty-three dollars," he said, "and thirty-two cents.
Now I can give you a hundred dollars credit, that's our maximum, and
as soon as you bring in your first furs we'll extend—"

He looked up then and he could not continue. The rage in
Johnson's face was like a hammer blow over his head: impossible to say
a word against. My god, Douglas thought. What's the matter with him?

Johnson's hand moved to his bulging coat pocket and Douglas had
a flash: something he had never thought behind his counter before: he's
pulling a gun on me! But it was simply a tobacco tin, a worn ordinary
tin of Macdonald's Fine Cut. Johnson placed it directly in front of him,
twisted the lid off with one broad hand and for a moment Douglas did
not know what he was looking at. He had never seen money on edge
like that: he realized he was looking at twenty-dollar bills, the can was
rolled tight with them.

Johnson closed the tin, put it back in his coat pocket, shifted his coat aside and pulled another roll of money out of his right pants pocket. One of the men behind him breathed heavily, like a sigh. Johnson took the rubber band off, began to peel fifty-dollar bills from the roll in slow deliberation. He counted out fifteen without a sound, laying them down in a row before Douglas like a card player laying his face cards out.

"Anybody trapping northwest of here," Johnson said to the quiet room, "along the Rat River?"

Douglas picked the bills up one by one, recovering slowly. "That's the Gwich'an country," he said finally. "Right to the mountains."

"No whites?"

Douglas finished counting and pulled out his drawer to make change.

"That's Indian country," he repeated. "You'll have to get a trapping licence from Corporal Millen anyways. He'll tell you."

"Licence?" Johnson's voice was startled. Douglas looked at him, offering the six dollars. For some reason the word "licence" had changed the look on Johnson's face.

"Your trap line here has to be registered in your name," Douglas said. "Millen started that. It saves a lot of quarrelling about who works where, and they know where you are."

Johnson looked at the trader deliberately, and slowly the stolid, immovable expressionlessness with which he had begun to buy his supplies settled on his rugged features. He ignored the change Douglas offered him. He turned to the trappers who had watched him silently, and he lifted his right fist. The thick roll was still in it.

"I want to buy a canoe," Albert Johnson said.

# 9

Grains of dry snow sprinkled out of the heavy sky as Millen wrote out William Nersyoo's trapping licence. October 17, 1931—and he did not have to ask where the big man's territory was; Nersyoo and his brother-in-law Peter Snowshoe had trapped northwest on the plateau below the Richardson Mountains, across the Rat and Barrier rivers for six years, carefully so as not to deplete the area but thoroughly too, taking the fox and mink and squirrel and rat steadily as they reproduced themselves.

"Okay." Millen handed over the paper. "And you even sold Knut some dogs you didn't need."

Nersyoo studied the lowering clouds. "If it'd snowed sooner," he said, "I'd have needed them, but I think we can still make it back in the canoe. Now."

"Yeah, it's sure easier than dragging a loaded sled over rocks," Millen said. "Let Knut worry about those pups tipping his canoe."

"I don't know," Nersyoo chuckled. "Knut's found someone he likes here. I don't think he's leaving too quick."

"Well," Millen said, "the winter's long enough, alone in bed."

"But maybe he can't get Noel Verville out of this one."

Millen laughed with Nersyoo, and then they both looked up the slope and saw Albert Johnson coming down from the trading post. Straight through the dead fire rings of the camp, an enormous load piled on his back and held in place by a tumpline across his forehead. He walked with sure, easy grace, the huge weight balanced on his hips and back, his rifle swinging lightly in his hand.

"Whew!" Millen said, amazed. "Two hundred and fifty pounds, at least."

"That's how they used to do it," Nersyoo said. "On the portages."

"You ever carry like that?" Millen asked.

But Nerysoo didn't answer. Because Johnson had come straight down towards the river past the heap of their packed camp and at that moment noticed Celeste Nerysoo sitting in the lee of it, nursing their baby. His head jerked towards her so that for an instant he seemed about to lose the rhythm of his movement and his look flashed at her, staring, livid as a flame, but actually he did not hesitate; his body with its hanging rifle and enormous square burden moved on down without a ripple to the big canoe sitting in the thin, smashed ice along the edge of the river.

Millen did not look at Nerysoo; he knew the Dene had seen that glance, but he did not, somehow could not, admit that he had seen it too. He found he was looking towards the distant shore, over the black-ish-grey water so visibly cold now he shivered, involuntarily, and he was thinking about the woman he had seen two months ago in Edmonton. When he had been out on leave and he had looked at her so hard, had seen her so suddenly, so intensely, that she had leaned away almost frightened. And said, finally, "Edgar, what is it?" Her delicate face so lovely, so close to him he was frightened too. An unexpected flash that showed too much.

A shriek and a thump on his leg: one small boy was chasing another and now Millen's long legs were the barrier, a temporary escape. He leaned over, scooped up chaser and chased and hung them from his hips like sacks of flour. They wriggled terrifically, in complete silence, while he ran heavily, jolting them hard, towards their family camp.

"No chasing anybody in my territory," he swung their heads up, nose to ruddy nose. "Or I'll throw you both in my jail!"

They laughed aloud at him then, squirming their small hard bodies like snakes until he could barely hold them.

Albert Johnson was loading his canoe. Very carefully, the way a single canoeist must so that the weight of his body will balance it and he can move straight across a wind or against a current with the least effort. His rifle was set against the edge of the canoe and he lashed the new shotgun and .22 Winchester he had bought to the thwarts on either side for balance. Then he stowed box after box of 30-30 bullets in a canvas sack, and he was tying it tight when a slight sound above him jerked his head up.

Millen stood there. Very tall, smiling and easy.

Johnson turned back to his loading. He tied the sack of ammunition to his seat webbing and then picked up a small framed window about a foot square, thoughtfully seemed to consider how he might fit that against the flour and rice sacks stowed near the front.

"That outfit should take you through the winter," Millen said.

Johnson shoved the window between sacks; he juggled it tightly into place, checking to see if any points could bring pressure against the glass. It seemed safe.

"I'm Spike Millen," the policeman said after a moment.

"Yeah," Johnson said finally, picking up a sack of clothing. "You control trapping licences."

"I wasn't thinking about that so much," Millen said, musing. "Last winter we had to make three extra patrols . . . you know, emergencies.

All at about thirty, forty below and seven, ten days round trip. One of the men we found had taken the top of his head off with his shotgun, one just like yours . . . another one wouldn't stop dancing. We had to rope him down in the dog sled, and when we untied him to eat he started dancing again. The third—"

Johnson had straightened up; his grey eyes narrow, clinched, met the policeman's deep blue ones.

"Don't worry," he said. "I've been alone fifteen years."

"When they came here," Millen said softly, "they wanted to be left alone too."

Johnson's mouth opened as if to retort, quickly, angrily, and then something twisted across his face and his head bent aside. He stooped, picked up the canvas lying on the splintered ice of the shore and spread it over the supplies in the canoe. He began to tie it down, intent on knots.

"Look," Millen said, calm and unruffled. "There's money here trapping, sure, if you know what you're doing."

"I've trapped," Johnson did not look up.

"What?"

"Mink. Squirrel and beaver." But the words seemed to loosen something in him and he continued almost fiercely, still bent down and fingers groping at the canvas, "People just get you in trouble, I've fished, farmed, trapped alone, I never—"

He broke off, as if he had said too much. His shoulders seemed to be shaking slightly.

Millen said after a long pause, "This is more fox and rat country."

But Johnson would not straighten up, would not face him. He was checking his knots, actually re-tying several, but his back remained bent as if he were muscling himself down low or else he would have to burst upright into a rage.

Millen said, carefully, "Anyway, alone in canyons of the Richardson Mountains is a little different from down south. There's more of everything, up here. Especially more alone."

"That's where Erickson went, to the mountains?"

"He went over them, into the Yukon. It'd be really tough to get that outfit through the Richardsons this late, there's only two routes, one up the Rat River and the other the Peel portage. That's shorter, but a lot of muskeg walking."

Except for his rifle, Johnson's canoe was packed. He picked the rifle up in his right hand and straightened to face Millen again. His expression was steady again, deliberately neutral; as if he had laid out all the parts of his face and body in implacable order.

Johnson said quietly, "I never said I wanted to get through the mountains."

"But I understand," Millen answered just as quietly, "you want to trap northwest, in the foothills by the Rat River."

They studied each other easily, Johnson holding the rifle motionless in his hand. Millen thought, a little more and I can maybe save myself a bad patrol, come on—and then Johnson's glance shifted away, over his shoulder. Hard, quick footsteps. It was Constable King coming down the slope; Millen could have cursed aloud but the moment was already gone. That was quite clear.

Johnson said, looking across the wide, muddy river steaming slightly in the cold, "Why are cops always so snoopy?"

"Well," Millen tried to keep his voice easy, as if considering a challenging philosophic question, "there's order. We're a community, pretty scattered but . . . community order depends on . . . a certain knowledge, a . . . common acceptance, say, of personal behaviour."

"I can't register," Johnson said between his teeth, "till I know where I'm trapping."

King said very loudly as he came up, "And how'll you trap anyway, without traps?"

"Al," Millen warned under his breath.

But whatever Johnson might have said was lost, now. He did not bother to look at either policeman again. He simply stepped through the slivered ice and nudged his laden canoe gently away from shore.

"There's plenty of room along the Rat River," Millen called after him, "especially higher in the mountains, near McDougall Pass. But you have to talk it over with the Indians on the river, William Nerysoo, Peter Snowshoe, where you trap. Okay?"

"Yeah," Johnson said. The canoe was afloat and he settled himself into it. He laid down his rifle carefully, picked up the paddle and with an expert thrust swung out into the river's current. He leaned into the water, hard, and quickly moved away.

"You ever heard of snares?" Millen said to King. "Deadfall maybe?"

"Douglas says he's got at least two thousand dollars on him," King justified himself quickly. "How—"

"Good," Millen said. "That keeps him free of Douglas's account book too."

"How would he get money like that?" King persisted. "Not with any goddamn snares. If he got that legally I'll—"

"Al," Millen said watching the canoe grow smaller, north, "if you're alone, there's nobody to waste it, spending it for you."

King looked at him, puzzled.

"Come on," Millen said heavily. He put his hand on his partner's shoulder and turned him up the slope moving with people. "We won't have another such a winter, not like last, I know it for sure."

"Yeah, yeah, I know," King grunted, walking. "You had your palm read."

"Did I tell you that?" Millen asked in mock astonishment.

"Just about every two days. Every time you get to Aklavik, Nurse Shirley takes your big hand in her little soft one and promises you every damn thing you want."

"Well, not quite everything, but I did try a new angle. I asked Mrs. Lindbergh if she might have a look, you know . . ."

King stopped, stared at him. "You asked Mrs. Lindbergh, to read your palm?"

"It took you so long to pump up that gas, I had to say something to keep her amused. The honour of the North, of the Force, you know."

"Good god, I bet! What did she say, huh?"

Millen said, deadpan, "She was very polite, polite but firm. Nothing if not firm. 'My dear corporal' . . . her exact words, Al, no bullshit . . . 'my dear corporal, if I could read palms, do you suppose I'd be flying around the world with Charles?'"

The two policemen roared with laughter; so loudly the canoeist in the middle of the river might have heard them. But he did not turn his head to look back.

*Part Two*

# The Sprung Trap

# 1

Dawn was a pale greyness outlining the shore shrubbery of Arctic spruce when Albert Johnson shoved his canoe through fresh slivered ice along the river gravel next morning. He had camped on a wooded spit where one twisted channel of the Rat River pushed its clear mountain water into the muddy Peel; today he was heading west.

Into the distant mountains. And here there was no more floating easy with an easy current. The short but turbulent Rat River, fanning down through the Mackenzie delta in three branches, ran fast over gravel between islands thick with willows and stunted spruce, curled tight against cut-mud banks in pools where the greyling hung motionless. As the sun rose higher he could see their silver bodies below him as he ploughed ahead, bending into his work in the calmer current against the shore, could see them twist and flicker away when the long shadow of his canoe touched them. The only sound was the mutter of the river, his comfortable grunts as he heaved ahead, and the occasional call of a raven on a dead spar watching him a moment before it lifted its great black body upward into air and sailed easily away, laughing. Or an eagle drifting, very high.

By noon the river was wider—he was now above where it fanned into its three branches on the delta—and so there was more water and less danger of gravel bars; but the river was climbing now. Towards its sources on the eastern slopes of the Richardson Mountains. At first its steps were small: sharp rock ledges where the water broke down like chuckling and he could step out onto rocks and pull the canoe, sometimes by the gunwale, sometimes by its lead rope, up and over with one massive lift into the quieter pool above. He did that again and again, working steadily and without stopping as it seemed he did everything, covering an amazing distance. For lunch he chewed dried meat but did not stop other than to paddle more slowly along a quiet bank. The ducks and geese were long gone, south.

The hills through which the river ran were higher here, bare, closing in, often cut in sharp banks against a bend, and suddenly he lifted his head, paused, listened. Ahead of him, beyond where he could see, the sound of the river changed, as if its voice had sunk down into itself. He put his shoulder down, paddled hard, and rounded the corner. A long, magnificent wash of white rapids between rocks rose above him, his head was filled with its deep, throaty roar.

Johnson stretched carefully. He could see the distant pyramids of mountains turning pale in the falling light, but the backward bend of boulders into white mist lay before him, the trees and rocks hanging everywhere brilliant with long dripping ice like a glistening canyon of spun glass. He sat for a moment, facing into that, and then he began to laugh. The river swallowed the sound as his tiny canoe turned slowly in the giant eddy below the final smooth slant of the rapids.

He was at the glistening junction of the Longstick and Rat rivers, at the rapids that had held gold-seeking Klondikers so long in 1898 that winter caught them before they could cross the Richardson Mountains to the Porcupine and Yukon rivers and along them to the gold diggings at Dawson City. The small debris of "Destruction City" as they called it, where some of the gold seekers froze and a few of them died, was still scattered along the tangled bush of the banks; but Johnson ignored it as he ignored the worn overgrown portage trail leading up through the brush. Instead, he pushed his canoe in under the left side of the rapids, checked all his packing to see that it was lashed down tight, then slung his rifle by its strap across his shoulder and stepped out onto a gravel bar. For a moment he studied the gleaming willowed banks above him, then he picked up the lead rope and began moving ahead. He stepped from rock to glazed rock, pulling the canoe after him through the swirling water. He was going to track the canoe along the length of the ice-hung rapids.

Sometimes he had to hack through willows, sometimes he was up to his waist in the tearing water and barely holding the weight of the canoe while he fought for balance, fought for the feel of an edged rock somewhere below to brace his feet and lever himself forward. Once it was the icy stripped limbs of a "sweeper" spruce that saved him being washed away completely: a few roots still gripped the bank though it had collapsed over the river and he clamped onto it just as his feet slipped, left the rocks and whipped up into the deadly give of water. He had the rope tied around his waist: that was very dangerous, but by then he had to use both hands to grab whatever was available and he clung to the gnarled tree, stretched by the ferocious current between that grey wood and the dead weight of his load. It seemed the water was viciously intent now to roll him under itself and down the rock ridges all the long distance he had laboured, smashed down to the bottom of the pool below.

He hung there, stretched, but gathering himself until slowly the power of his long arms and stomach asserted itself and he tightened forward onto that beautiful stripped tree, could hold himself against the rope and level his feet down with nothing but his stomach muscles to force them down—they whipped up again—down, down to solid rock bottom, at last. After that it was easy getting up on the safety of the boulders, so close but unreachable all the time he was stretched out there. He could pause then, force himself ahead on the jagged rocks even if it meant ramming up through ice-crusted brush, trusting his icy feet to the water. On and on he struggled, and finally he saw ahead of him the quiet river, levelled like a lake into the tight valley ahead. He staggered out on a small sand wedge, heaved the canoe up and, soaked as he was, collapsed there. His stomach and chest heaved in the sharp cold air. In a moment he was asleep flat on his back, his right arm flung over his eyes, and smiling.

And in another moment startled awake. It was not because his clothes were slowly freezing over his body; it was because above the steady drone of rapids below he had heard a foreign sound—a growl. But when he jerked up, already swinging the rifle around, he saw only a single caribou across the narrow river from him, splashing through the shallows towards a gravel bar. An old bull, his throat hung with long white fur, and so exhausted he seemed barely able to lift his huge rack of antlers. As soon as he reached the gravel he turned back towards the bank, squaring around, and the long gaping slashes on his heaving flank showed then, the blood spread wide down his leg.

"The wolves had a go at you," the man muttered aloud. "Poor old bugger."

Out of the willow brush on the bank came a grizzly. Head down, broad shaggy body set on legs like bowed pillars, smelling the blood spoor and then raising its snout to growl again as it saw the caribou standing on the open gravel too exhausted to try swimming the swift river. The bear growled again, menacing, its pointed tan-brown head swinging from side to side like a snake, glaring across the shallow water at the old bull standing in his classic defence posture, back legs spread, braced, and his five-foot antlers lowered squarely down. Then out of the brush tumbled a grizzly cub, and another: both bleating loudly. The big bear whipped her head around at them an instant, growled, and they scrambled back to the edge of the brush, silent now and watching.

The bull had outrun the wolves, but he could run no further. Johnson lifted his rifle.

But he did not shoot. He himself had crawled up out of the white dismal canyon of the rapids, a canoe with all his winter supplies tied to his waist, and here a hundred yards across water too fast for any animal to swim without being swept away there emerged this ultimate meeting between antlers and claws. It comes when it comes. He sat in his frozen clothes, his rifle poised, watching.

The grizzly sow paced along her bank, head low and weaving; the caribou bull across the strip of water stood like a planted statue. Only his delicate head with its magnificent curved-forward antlers moved always to face her. Back and forth, back and forth. His nostrils wide as he gasped for air; always facing her. The cubs crouched against the brush and bawled plaintively; the sow wheeled on hind legs, long fur whipping in an arc and for an instant it seemed she would charge, but she did not: she was padding back again, her small fierce head on her long neck snaking back and forth.

"You can handle her," Johnson muttered. "Sure."

The grizzly charged. Crashing into the water and the bull's head dropped until his flaring nose was against the stones and the four giant stems of his antlers with their blades and shovels and prongs confront-ed her like a wall of spikes. Through the water she came, spray flying and her mouth one huge roar of teeth and with perfect timing the bull rammed his rack into her chest, his great haunches driving him forward so that the crusted wounds on his flanks burst open in a bright spray of blood. And he stopped her, solid, rammed her upright on her haunches so that for an instant they stood as if carved from shaggy stone: the caribou braced forward, the grizzly erect on her back legs, caught upright and suspended with the power of her charge.

"That's it!" the man muttered.

And then the bull was forcing her back. His splayed hoofs gouged the gravel, he was heaving her backward into the shallow water with the two lower branches of his antlers driving into her chest. She staggered back, jerking, she might fall over backward, but her forepaws were free, her head untouched and high above his; between the magnificent curve of his upper rack her powerful neck and shoulders arched in roar after roar and her right paw swung through hard, caught against his upper horn and with blow upon blow she hammered the caribou off his feet, over into the stream. There was a flurry of water, stiff splayed legs and hoofs waving desperately in the unresisting air, and then the grizzly was on top, shoulder muscles heaving as her head worked down lower and lower into the water. The white wash of their wrestling abruptly ran red.

Albert Johnson shivered. He was still sitting there, tense, with his rifle up and he looked at it in a kind of wonder before he dropped it in his lap. After a moment he began to break the ice out of his pants, cuffing them lightly, flakes falling on the black sand. Then, ponderously like an old tired man, he got to his feet.

The grizzly sow was hauling the caribou carcass towards the river bank. The half-grown cubs were at the water's edge, bleating, scrambling over each other in their excitement.

Johnson went forward, bent to untie his axe from his canoe packing. He looked around a moment, made up his mind about the heavy willow brush and spruce on the bank behind him, and the fine hard sand of the spit under his feet, ribbed and frozen dry. He started working on the lashings of his tent. The cubs were making small dashes into the water as the carcass surged closer.

"Never smile at a woman," Johnson half sang under his breath. "Call no man your friend. If you trust anybody, you'll be sorry . . . you'll be sorry . . . you'll be sorry, in the end."

# 2

JUST AFTER NOON THE NEXT DAY Johnson found the place he wanted in the narrowing valley of the Rat River.

Well before dawn he had broken camp, the grizzlies across the river concerned only with their feeding and still totally oblivious of him, and paddled past them upstream. The sow was lying on her back just then, resting or perhaps sleeping. The cubs were busy nursing, tugging at her dugs between her vicious claws that waved gently as wings in the air above them. A tumble of teddy bears, really, except for the mangled carcass of the caribou at the stream's edge beside them.

Eight miles up the river, which here generally ran south in many small channels, he found the promontory. It lay open in a bend of water, sixty strides across with low bushy banks on three sides and a stand of spruce on the fourth. The straggly spruce were large enough, the visibility clear in every direction except the trees and the farther reaches of the Richardson plateau and foothills and ultimate mountains beyond them already bright with snow.

He shifted his rifle to his left hand, stooped, picked up a stick and looked around. The clearing was level, empty; grains of snow were falling out of the grey sky, blurring the white blunt pyramids on the skyline. He moved a few feet to his left and dropped the stick; looked around again to all sides, then placed his foot on it.

Except for a faint murmur from the river, he stood in complete silence.

# 3

BY THE END OF NOVEMBER the spruce, the clearing on the promontory, and the new cabin in it facing east down the bent, frozen river were all deep under snow. Days had grown very short now, no more than two hours of low sunlight and then a steady fade of light along the horizon into darkness by the early afternoon, but the snow was still light, puffed up and layered as in early fall, not whipped flat into the hard drifts of winter.

Johnson had been very lucky with the snow, building his cabin so late. He was just now fitting a narrow door into the door space, the untanned moose hide he had been using flung aside on the snow. The door was thick planks, each axed out of a single length of spruce, and the opening to the cabin was down inside a hole dug a foot into the snow and almost two feet into the perma-frost. The slope-roofed cabin stood only four feet above the snow in front, three feet at the back: he had built the walls very low and then hacked out the centre of the cabin to give headroom. With the thawed dirt piled on the sapling roof, the cabin was far warmer than anything set at ground level, and by fitting the low door half into the earth too, almost all draught there would be eliminated.

He pounded nails through doubled moose-hide hinges into the logs beside the tiny window. He was using the blunt end of his axe to do so, steel on steel cracking sharp in the cold. He hunched forward on the steps he had cut into the frozen earth and pounded the lower nails in also. The door swung nicely, but jammed along the side. He was shaving off curls of spruce with his axe blade when he heard a dog yelp.

Deliberately he pushed the door shut, jammed it tight, and came up out of the doorhole with his axe still in his hand. The hard sunlight of noon was bright with glare on the frozen river, upstream, he could see a dog team coming there, and a man running behind it. He shaded his eyes, watched a moment, then picked up the rifle leaning against the wall by the window and pushed through the soft snow to the woodpile in the lee of the cabin. He set the rifle against the logs and began to split wood on his chopping block. He swung steadily, deliberately, and with every swing his head came up to glance at the approaching team.

The driver yelled and the lead dog wheeled left, pulling the four tandem-hitched dogs behind him like a string towards the promontory. For a moment they were gone below the bank, only their yelps flicking in the frozen air as the driver shouted, cracking his whip, and then they burst over the edge with the loaded sled heaving up out of the snow behind them and the driver scrambling after with the balance rope in his hand, trying to keep the sled from tipping. The dogs were slaver-mouthed with excitement, charging onto the clearing with snow flying, but well trained too for when the driver swung his long whip over them and yelled, they slowed immediately, then stopped in front of Johnson who was leaning on his axe now, without any motion whatever.

The long snow-splattered sled was heavily loaded, and at the very back sat a Dene woman holding a wrapped bundle in her arms that could only be a baby. The driver, Dene as well, tossed his curled whip on the load and looked up. He was breathing white clouds from the run, but smiling in the sharp sunlight.

"Hello," he said. He took a step forward and stopped. Johnson said nothing. "I saw you at Fort McPherson," the man said.

It was William Nerysoo. Johnson had not heard his name there, he did not ask it now, and the Dene would never offer it. After a moment Johnson said, "Hello."

His voice was so deliberately neutral that Nerysoo looked at him with a quick glance of wonder. Johnson's axe was butted on the chopping block.

"Nice cabin," Nerysoo said after a moment, looking around.

Johnson was studying the woman. She was seated easily for the ride in the rough bouncy sled, as if balanced in a cupped hand, and the child in her lap was obviously sleeping through it all bundled up tight and warm against the cold. At her left elbow, beside the coiled whip was tied a sheathed rifle with an inch of its butt protruding.

"You live here now?" Nerysoo asked.

"Yeah," Johnson said. And, after a moment, "Good place for winter."

Within the wolverine-fur circle of her parka, Celeste Nerysoo's downcast face was like a cameo: a man could easily imagine how beautiful the rest of her body must be.

"Yeah," Nerysoo said, "good place to see all around, see what's coming."

Johnson's glance broke away from the woman and he stared intently at the tall Dene.

"In case a moose walks by," he said, hard.

And suddenly he laughed, loudly, and in an instant Nerysoo had joined him. They both looked around the promontory, just in case a moose were walking by, and their laughter bounced off the icy spruce. When they stopped, very abruptly, the echo of their echo mumbled at them from across the bent river.

"We People," Nerysoo said after a moment, and paused. His voice was warm and easy as between friends, "We never live alone." He laughed a little. "A wife is very good, good to talk, work skins, real warm at night, good on the trap line, this country's cold enough. . . ."

He laughed again. "Kids real good too. Family."

But Johnson did not respond. He was looking off somewhere upriver, his face set again as if there were no one in the clearing with him. Nerysoo glanced around, uncomfortably. The Savage 30-30 rifle leaned against the woodpile; he bent down, picked it up.

Celeste in the sled saw his movement and her face stiffened with fear.

Nerysoo held the rifle high, away from him in his two mittened hands. The rifle was very light, and tapered smoothly from the thick stock and bulge of its trigger-guard to the tip of its barrel like a short lunging spear; its wood was smooth to the grain like the palm of a worn hand. Nerysoo took off one mitten and set the rifle on his finger; it balanced there, perfect. He looked up at Johnson with a grin.

Johnson's grey eyes were studying him; there was no expression whatever on his face.

Nerysoo fit the rifle to his shoulder. On the western edge of the clearing a spruce stump stuck out of the snow, a narrow strip of bark peeled down its side: a very small target. Nerysoo's eye caught Johnson's across the rear sight.

"Try it," Johnson said.

"Loaded?"

"All the time."

Nerysoo lowered the rifle, cocked it. His lead dog sat up, looking at him keenly, and he spoke a quiet Dene word. The dog sank down in the snow again. But Nerysoo did not see his wife huddled down in the sled now, clutching their baby. He was aiming across the length of the clearing. Carefully; and then he fired.

The dogs leaped to their feet. He spoke sharply to them, cocked the rifle and fired at the stump again, much quicker this time. The gunshot echoed and re-echoed in the hard bright cold.

"You hit both," Johnson said.

Nerysoo was smiling, handing him the rifle. "A real good one."

The dogs were very nervous now, almost shivering though still seated in their tracks. Suddenly a squirrel chattered in the nearest trees. Johnson wheeled, had cocked and thrown up the rifle in seemingly the same motion and fired at the instant the rifle came up level with his shoulder. A splotch of brown on a shaking branch exploded into red as the shot crashed farther and farther down the valley behind them.

Nerysoo stood staring at the branch, the fragments of the blasted squirrel, in stunned amazement.

The dogs, strangely, sank back into the hollows of their bodies in the snow. Celeste had begun to tug at the rifle tied to the sled but she shrank down now, lower as if she would disappear, clutching the bundle of her child even tighter.

Johnson dropped his slightly smoking rifle into the crook of his arm.

"My trap line," Nerysoo explained after a long moment, when he had re-arranged his face, "it's across the river here." He gestured east downstream in the direction they were going. "My grandfather, my father, we always trapped here, my sister and brother-in-law are up there a little ways," he moved his hand upstream, still without looking at Johnson, "there by the little spring, they cross there."

"I built my place here, I never bother nobody," Johnson said in his thin, hard voice. "If they don't bother me."

Nerysoo glanced at him quickly, and their eyes met. Then the Dene turned to go, but stopped after one step in the snow. The clearing in the wilderness was so silent they heard the wings of a raven swish deep in the spruce behind them.

"Where do you come from?" Nerysoo said fast, without looking up.

Such a stunningly personal question for a Dene to ask a white, beside his own cabin: Johnson's unbendable expression wavered; almost as if he would have to acknowledge some information, something vital to his past. He opened his mouth slowly.

"You saw me," he said like iron. "Down the river."

Nerysoo would not look back at the other man. After a long moment he trudged heavily to his sled.

"Lots of white men," he said, "come down the river. They always come from some place."

He was picking up his coiled whip when he noticed the expression on Celeste's face. She sat hunched under the covering hides, her eyes wide open to him in the glare of sunlight and dilated with fear.

Nerysoo hesitated, then swung his whip hand up like an assault, the whip exploding as he shouted to his dogs. They leaped up, and the leader quickly swung them around into the track they had come. The huge wheel dog hauled the sled around so sharply Nerysoo had to lunge for the trailing balance rope and heave the end of the sled over or it would have spilled sideways in the powdery snow.

Johnson watched his first visitors grow small on their own trail back up the Rat River; not downstream as they had come, but headed back for brother-in-law Peter Snowshoe. The rifle in the crook of Johnson's arm moved round and round in a small rhythm so that the black hole of the muzzle traced a slow O in the brittle air.

# 4

A FIRE OF SPLIT SPRUCE burned in the corner fireplace. Within the small circle of its light, Johnson was doing a Dene woman's work, weaving moose-hide thongs across snowshoe frames. He worked steadily, his blunt fingers threading the holes he had burned through pointed willow frames in patterns, through and over, tying the hide at the junctures in flip knots over itself. He was almost to the line of webbing where the heel of his foot would fit: at the middle crossbar of the heavy wood. He tied another tight knot, and stopped.

He stared into the fire. The yellow light of it threw his seated shadow on the wall behind him, frosty earth and thick, chinked logs.

He put the snowshoe down beside the other one, already completely webbed, got up and stooped to the left side of the fireplace. A tunnel had been dug there, at right angles into the earth. He knelt down and crawled into it, and for a moment only the firelight flickered in the tiny cabin, laying a warm yellow glow over the blankets and hides unrolled in one corner, around the low earth and log walls, the black glassy stare of the tiny window beside the oblong of the door so white and startling in the general darkness. There was a shuffle of boxes from the tunnel, and then Johnson re-emerged into the firelight. He held three bullets in his hand.

The 30-30 stood upright beside the fireplace, between the .22 rifle and the shotgun. He reloaded it, put it back in its place. A few cooking utensils sat there also in a neat pattern, a frying pan and a tin pail of water. Johnson stooped before the fire, staring downward the way a person does when he is not seeing anything at his feet, then slowly he sat down on the stool again and his hand came up, reached to his shirt pocket.

He was looking at a picture in his spread hand tilted to the fire. A grainy black and white snapshot of a fishing boat tied to a plank pier with other smudges of boat around it. In the distance, beyond white squares of houses, rose the outline of mountains. A seaport, perhaps Vancouver, or San Francisco, its details clearer at a distance than when brought close. But Johnson set the picture directly in the firelight under his nose, and he was peering at the two men on the deck of the boat. One was young, slim in fisherman's clothing—it might have been Johnson himself as a young man—and hanging slanted by one hand from the single mast and waving happily, a huge smile on his face. Beside him, very erect and stiff, stood a man of much the same shape, though clearly older for he wore no cap on his white hair. He stood solid, legs apart and arms rigid, grim, without any gesture whatever.

Johnson shifted his hand and now two pictures lay side by side: the one of the fishing boat and another. This one showed what was probably a backyard garden of flowers, huge puffs of lighter and darker sprays of blossoms whose colour it was impossible to deduce from the grainy greyness but with the same high skyline stretched above the picket fence, and the same young man leaning against it still very nonchalant and happy, though not waving. Dressed in the square dress uniform of a sailor, perfectly groomed and at ease in his world.

He had been studying the pictures so intently in the thick light that his eyes watered. He sat back a moment, eyes closed, and then looked at his hand again. Half revealed there now lay a third picture, a diagonal of a young woman's hair, eye, half a nose and lips between the two pictures he had studied so carefully; but when he saw that he shoved them together quickly, like a card player discarding useless cards, and thrust all three away again into his shirt pocket.

He stood up then, took a round box from the ledge over the fireplace, twisted it open and shook two pills into his hand. He dropped them in his mouth and leaned against the fireplace for a moment with them on his tongue. The light from below his sharp weathered face with its high widow's peak of light brown hair staggered his profile against the pole ceiling. Then he bent to the water pail, lifted it, and drank.

"You'll be sorry in the end," he muttered at the snapping fire.

# 5

ALBERT JOHNSON STOOD on his snowshoes beside the sloping bank of the Rat River. He raised a heavy stick, the kind of stick a man uses to test the ice ahead of him when he is walking a creek or river. He seemed about to plunge the stick into the snow, but hesitated. He looked behind him.

Up the level river, silver like steel in the cold, his cabin under its covering of driven snow was clearly visible on the promontory.

He turned, jabbed the stick into the drift against the bank. The jaws of a large steel trap snapped up out of the snow, clamped around the stick. He jerked the trap out completely, traced its chain to its anchor in the ice and cleared the snow away. Carefully, working without haste or anger, he cracked free the end of chain frozen there. Then he hung the trap, with the stick still in its teeth, over a willow leaning from the river bank. Very plainly; no one coming along the frozen river could help but notice it.

# 6

FOR A QUIET MOMENT Spike Millen stared at the trap with the heavy stick in its jaws. Then up at William Nerysoo, who had placed it so quietly on his desk blotter.

"How do you know it was him?" Millen asked finally.

"His snowshoe tracks," Nerysoo said. "He just sprung it, hung it up and went right back to his cabin."

"One trap?"

"Yeah."

Nerysoo bent forward, pulled his outer parka off over his head.

"You got it nice and warm in here," he said shrugging his inner caribou clothes back in place.

Millen looked across the trap at the tiny spruce perched on the corner of his desk, at the small tracery of silver and red streamers woven around it. Christmas, he thought. The best time of the winter, and the worst time too, the toughest men often snapped then—or whenever they decided it was Christmas on their makeshift calendars.

"He hasn't laid out a trap line himself?"

"I never saw nothing, anywhere," Nerysoo said, loosening his shirt collar.

"Then what's he doing there, huh?"

Nerysoo shrugged, grinning slightly. "What do white men do, all alone?" he said.

Millen laughed aloud, but not happily. "Especially at Christmas," he muttered to himself. "How many traps have you got on the Rat River?"

"Six or seven," Nerysoo said. And after a moment of silence, "That's one of the best places, along there, for fox. And spring rats."

"I know, I know. And Peter's trapping upstream there too?"

"Yeah."

"Well, if Johnson's not trapping . . ." Millen hesitated.

Nerysoo looked at him steadily. Two families, eight people. One trap today, two tomorrow, if he imagined the whole Rat was his . . . there was no way around it.

"Okay Bill," Millen's tone changed, "we'll look into it. Al!" he called.

Alfred King's tousled brown head appeared at the inside door.

"We'll start our patrol north tomorrow, but do the Rat River loop first."

King walked into Millen's small office, his mouth hanging open. "Tomorrow? My god, Spike, it's Christmas Day!"

"Oh," Millen seemed to remember, though he was grinning at Nerysoo, "so it is. Then I guess we'll just have to wait till Boxing Day."

King stood there with such incredulity on his face that first Millen and then Nerysoo burst out laughing.

"Don't you know any RCMP history, Al?" Millen asked. "For fifteen years the Fort McPherson-Dawson City patrol was always on the trail over Christmas. It's a proud tradition. Ignoring all times and seasons the RCMP proudly plod forward on their duty."

"Yeah, I know, I know," King said grimly, "and I also know what happened to Inspector Fitzgerald and his men on that 1911 patrol."

"Bill," Millen said, "you'll have to tell King the Indian version of what happened to Fitzgerald."

"Doesn't matter who tells the story," Nerysoo said. "All of them froze."

"But why?" King said. "Why, eh?"

"Let's not get morbid," said Millen, "after twenty years. It sure wasn't because of Christmas." He gestured to the trap on his desk. "We've just got a bit of trap-line business to clear up."

"Johnson?" King asked quickly.

"Yeah," Nerysoo said. "On the best part of my line."

King gave Millen a glance.

"All right, all right," Millen said, conceding part of the disagreement they had had since Johnson paddled away in October. "One trap, one question will clear it up."

"Sure," King said slowly to Nerysoo. "We'll go out and talk to him, day after tomorrow. We were going out anyway on our northern patrol, in four days."

# 7

THERE WAS NO DAYLIGHT NOW. The continuous Arctic night turned into a grey southern lightness at noon, a suggestion of sun perhaps beyond the pall of dingy overcast, and the wind from the northwest moaned low and fierce, working at the ridged and rifted snow. It was thirty-seven degrees below zero when Millen and King left Fort McPherson on Saturday, December 26, 1931; they drove their two teams straight north up the Peel River and camped for the night in the shelter of low spruce at the mouth of the frozen Rat. The snow was so crusted they needed no trail breaker; they had made thirty miles, very good for a first day's run. Towards night the wind dropped and the windchill softened to about seventy degrees below zero. Still enough to freeze spit before it hit the snow, or exposed flesh in thirty seconds.

But the clouds cleared. As Millen rolled over tight in his eider bag beside the fire he could see stars, and then gradually a moving strip of orange and red northern lights rose brilliant as a banner, flaming up in the east. He watched that a moment, it was dying down again like strange, heavenly fire quenched softly by a hand. The cold gnawed at his face; across the campfire King's shape lay motionless, perhaps already asleep. Millen pulled the hood of his bag over, tight. A good start to a patrol with a good companion who knew his job, all ten dogs strong and no fights among them yet, and tomorrow it would probably be a bit colder but maybe no wind to face into climbing west up the Rat: temperature was always easier to handle than wind. His bag was as tight and warm as a cocoon. Almost like the quilt and the woman tight along him, long smooth and grainy under his finger tips. Edmonton, his father bumping a wide broom down a school corridor. "Men are made funny," she said, "so soft and hard in the same place." He shifted his hips and shoulder down into the spruce branches. Less memory than living dream; twenty-four-hour Arctic night around numberless fires like this and running, running, the endless frozen white of white, sheer running, he was already asleep.

Daylight was only a thin slit of brightness next day at noon when his mittened fist knocked on the new door. He waited, and listened. He could hear nothing. He bent down and knocked again, more loudly.

"Mr. Johnson," he called, "this is Spike Millen from Fort McPherson."

There was no sound. He studied the tiny window: it was the one he had seen Johnson pack tight in his canoe. Yes. A hide hung inside, nothing there. He glanced up at the smoke lifting away from the tin stove-pipe into the fierce, bright cold, and then he crunched down into the door-well and pulled at the door. It was tight, bolted inside.

"Mr. Johnson?"

King came wading around a drifted corner from behind the cabin.

"A real tight place," he said through the hoar of his parka fur. "Double walled, low and solid, built just about like a fort."

Millen looked up at him, puzzled. "I can't hear a thing, and it's closed from inside. Maybe he's sick in there."

King grimaced hugely against the cold, loosening his face muscles. "Maybe he's sleeping off his Christmas turkey," he muttered, sarcastic, and bent down and hammered on the door.

"Johnson! We want to ask you some questions. Open up!"

Millen jerked his arm up to stop him, and then he stiffened: a large hand was dropping a corner of the moose hide back inside the window.

"He's in there all right," King said very quietly.

Millen knocked his ordinary knock. "Mr. Johnson," he called. "Are you all right?"

There was absolute silence. From the spruce came the ominous squawk of a raven and one of the dogs growled in reply, behind them.

"We have a complaint about you," Millen continued, "and all I want is to hear your explanation."

The silence continued. After a moment King moved restlessly in the snow. "Let's kick the damn door down," he muttered.

Millen glanced up at him swiftly; that didn't deserve comment. He bent to the door.

"Mr. Johnson," he said slowly against the planks, "now listen carefully. We're cold, and we're going to build a fire below on the river and boil tea. Just come out when you're ready, and give us your explanation, and we'll be off. We've still got a long patrol to make."

"The bastard," King growled, turning away and cuffing his hands about his chest to get warm.

In an hour even the low brightness was gone; they had made their tea in the partial shelter of the curved river bank, but Johnson had not come. His cabin sat on the darkening promontory, half driven over by drifts and staring at them with its one tiny window glazed in the final bits of light, its smoke drifting up into the now-motionless cold.

Millen took another long sip of steaming tea. King came from where the dogs stirred on their chains in the gloom beyond the fire and drew off a mitt.

"My wheel dog's got one flank rubbed raw already," he said. "I'll have to change him for a few days."

"That stretch up the broken ice didn't help," Millen said, pouring him a cup from the black tin in the fire. "Can he lead?"

"Not as good as Tip." King hunched down, took a long slurp, then looked up at the drifted bank. From down beside the fire they could see only the cabin's vanishing smoke.

"Why don't you get the grub out," Millen said, getting up. "We'll sleep here and continue up the river at midnight. Should be a good running moon."

"What about him?" King gestured.

Millen pulled on his mitts.

"I'll go and have a little chat with him now," he said.

King pushed himself to his feet. "I better come along."

"No," Millen said. "Just get the food ready."

"Spike, he doesn't talk, he's loaded with money, he won't even open his damn door to warm us up in this ball-freezing—"

"Al," Millen said, and King stopped abruptly. There is only one man in command on any RCMP patrol, but that alone would not have stopped the big constable so quickly. Every day they worked and lived together; it was the two months that they had allowed their original disagreement about Johnson to sit wordlessly between them. It was Millen's way of being a policeman, which wasn't King's way, and after a year of Arctic life together they both knew it very well. It was Millen's easy-going and deliberate personal authority, totally immovable once fixed, in contrast to King's quick aggressive insistence on law: you did not argue these things, insofar as they were arguable, on a long and always potentially dangerous winter patrol. Not even when a subordinate thought a commanding officer was making a bad decision; as had happened on the Fitzgerald patrol in 1911. If absolutely necessary you wrote a separate report when the patrol was over; if you got back. But always there was that necessary order between men, especially in the Christmas darkness of the Arctic. King hunched down and drank his tea; Millen scrambled up the bank.

The clearing of the promontory was drifted, badly, but the drifts here were not yet strong enough to support a man's weight without snowshoes, as they were on the river. Millen broke through with one foot, and drove through with the next heaving his leg out and he cursed his carelessness in not putting on his shoes, but he would not go back now and have King face him blackly again. The dark hulk of the cabin was only thirty yards from the bank: he ploughed on, breath snoring in his chest, and rested for a moment looking at the front entrance. Low, excellently built to handle the cold. Another storm or two and it would be drifted over: let him hibernate like any sour old bear and come out in spring when the sunshine and spring water finally soaked and softened him up . . . poor bastard whatever his problem; and he stepped forward quickly and bent to the door.

"Mr. Johnson," he said, knocking carefully. "It's Spike Millen again. Will you talk to me?"

He listened so hard he could hear his heavy breathing move his chest; but there was no sound from inside. It was so unnaturally quiet that it was impossible that beyond the pale door someone was not listening. He stepped down and sat down deliberately in the door-well.

"Listen," he said loudly. "What you did is the trapper's way of saying, 'You're trespassing on my territory.' But you're wrong about that. That was William Nerysoo's trap and it was on his registered trap line. So you have to explain yourself."

The ravens suddenly burst into a racket among the spruce: almost as if one of them had awakened from a nightmare. Millen waited, but nothing else stirred.

"If you're not trapping," Millen continued after a moment, "it doesn't matter to me you never came back to file for a licence. I think there's enough caribou and probably moose around here for you and all the Indian people. But Nerysoo's a good man in a large, hard-working family and he's never bothered anyone . . . huh," he snorted, thinking of it, "we ought to have more like him, keep all of Fort McPherson going a little better. Why'd you spring his trap?"

.    He waited again. The individual planks of the door were becoming clearer: moonlight rising already. He shifted in the snow; one sometimes talked for days to men totally silent across a campfire after running nine or ten hours breaking trail ahead of a dog team. Faces like worked stone. And suddenly a word would fall, you never knew when.

"You think I don't want to leave you alone? Huh! Half the people who come north want to be left alone. Mostly they're running away from the south, or east or west, wherever," he laughed a little, ruefully. "You know what I ran away from? Smiling for the cameras. The great Canadian RCMP, famous for their scarlet uniforms and nice solid-chin smiles. All the rich tourists, the ones who can still afford to sip mint juleps behind the fence on the verandah of the Chateau Lake Louise, and there's plenty, clicking away and me with my hands folded behind my famous red jacket. Smiling. And then the special assignments to Calgary to hammer the souplines of unemployed men into order. Either that or writing reports, forms piled higher and deeper, bull."

He almost stood up to kick at the snow, but the implacable plank door faced him.

"You have to talk a little bit, Johnson," he said, exasperated. "You can't just refuse . . . that's what makes people human—they talk to each other. It makes us different from animals. Animals either just leave each other alone, up north anyway, or they kill each other. The Inuit told me that long ago, when I first got here. 'If we couldn't talk and dance and sing,' they said one winter when we'd been dancing about four days straight, 'we wouldn't be people any more. The land and the long darkness is too much here.' And they're right, you know, they're right."

The moon was quite bright now, the temperature dropping: he could feel it on his face, the prickle in his motionless feet. He waited and waited, finally he stood up in the door-well.

"You know what you're making us do? King and I'll have to chase our dogs back to McPherson forty-five miles in this forty below weather and I'll write a report to my Inspector, Eames in Aklavik, on a form they've got printed to explain why I had to swear out a search warrant on you, and then King and I will come back in probably worse weather and kick your door down. You want that?"

There was nothing but the door confronting him with its absolutely silent, unmoving blankness.

"You're not making a good new year for yourself," Millen said heavily. Then he turned and trudged away through the breaking drifts. "Or me."

The very thought of the gut-wrenching distance back to Fort McPherson, running all the way to save the dogs, left him no energy even to curse.

# 8

ONE LONG GRUELLING DRIVE LATER Millen was bent over paper at his desk, writing with swift, furious strokes. King pushed through the side door like a mobile arsenal, four Lee-Enfield rifles in his arms, four service revolvers hanging in holsters over his shoulders.

"A lot of trappers coming in for New Year's Eve," he said. "Knut Lang's back, Verville, a couple of the Firth and Snowshoe brothers—"

"That's plenty," Millen growled. "Two of them can volunteer."

King began ratching the bolt action of each rifle with great care. "It's too cold," he said calmly, "and too damn far not to prepare for any eventuality."

"I'm explaining all that, to Inspector Eames here," Millen said sarcastically, glancing up at King's steady racket with the rifles. "Sidearms, rifles, special constables—"

He stopped himself as William Douglas entered just then, long official papers in his winter-red hands.

"Here's the warrant," he said, "ready for oath and signature. Break in and search, as necessary."

Millen pulled a Bible out of his desk quickly. He had not even bothered to remove his trail clothes.

"You might as well sleep in your bed one night," the old trader said kindly, looking at his stubbled face. "If Johnson's gone when you get there, you're rid of your problem."

"He can start others," Millen growled. "It's a long winter."

# 9

BUT GREY SMOKE STILL ROSE from the cabin on the promontory when they pulled up under the river bank where the ashes of their first fire had drifted over. Leaving Fort McPherson at midnight and using Knut Lang's and Noel Verville's fresh teams on the now well-worn trail, they had driven straight through and arrived by two in the afternoon of December 29, just as the last light was fading over the river. Verville staked out the dogs and Millen went up the bank to study the cabin.

"That's one of the rules," King said to Lang, unwrapping the Lee-Enfields from one sled. "The Mounted Police never shoot first."

Lang worked the bolt of one rifle twice, then slowly began to shove in long tapered bullets one by one. "In the war," he said in his rising accent, "I shoot at lots of men, but," he laughed a little, "I never know if I hit anything. I shoot and duck, quick, that's all."

"I've been with the police five years," King said in his humourless way, "and I've never shot at a man yet."

Millen came crunching back, and Verville from the dogs among the willows. King handed the Metis trapper an unloaded rifle.

"And you won't have to shoot today either," Millen said. "Knut and Noel, you stay below here, spread apart a bit below the bank. And remember, you do not shoot unless Al or I give you the signal. You're strictly a precaution."

"Sure," Lang said, and Verville nodded, loading.

"I have a feeling," Millen began quietly to King, and hesitated.

"What'd you see up there?" King asked.

"Oh . . . nothing, it's just like before, smoke and not a thing moving, like nobody'd ever lived here."

"He's there," King said peering over the bank.

"I know that," Millen said quickly, "but I just feel I should go up there, alone."

King looked at him steadily. They were below the lip of the river bank and on either side the two trappers were moving into position with their police rifles.

"Spike," King said hard, "we've run over a hundred miles for that warrant in the dead of winter and sworn in two special constables and you've written your report and we're doing this by the rules now."

"Rules are for Regina classrooms."

King looked through the hoar of his parka at Millen without a word. A wide, implacable face; reports and more and more conflicting reports.

"Okay," Millen said finally. "Okay. Carry your rifle so Johnson can see it. Come on."

"You got your revolver?"

"You got yours?" Millen said tightly, going. King patted his parka. "Okay. I don't carry anything Johnson can't see."

"You trust that—" King burst out, and checked himself.

"Al," Millen said, patient now, "we've got three rifles on him."

He wheeled and stepped up over the bank, pulling papers from inside his parka and sorting them. He stood then in plain view of the cabin, pushing several papers back into his pocket and holding one in his mittened hand. King came up holding his rifle low before him with both hands.

"Mr. Johnson!" Millen shouted suddenly. "Will you come out and talk? If not, we have a warrant here to enter your cabin. By force, if necessary!"

New snow had fallen overnight and, protected by the green fringe of spruce behind it, the tiny cabin had not been as driven over with drifts as Millen had expected. Rather, its roof was flounced almost cockily under thick snow, and the pale smoke curling gently up from its stub chimney into the cloudless blue sky made it seem a fairy place, a gnome's retreat perhaps in the steely white, but strangely soft and curled too, peaceful world of winter. There was not a single sound or movement to disturb it: the two policemen tall and obtrusive on the bank waited, waited.

Millen said finally, "Come on."

They ploughed straight across the clearing side by side. Gradually King separated himself to the right, the door side, so that when they arrived at the cabin, panting from the soft snow, Millen with his paper

RCMP approaching Albert Johnson's cabin

looked down directly into the tiny window while King with his rifle half up was right of the door-well. Footprints led in and out on the steps, certainly made after the night's snow, around towards the woodpile. Millen nodded to King and bent down, stared at the window.

There was no moose hide behind it now. Only the wedge of light like a square column down into the darkness inside, down to the earth floor—empty—with the distorted reflection of his own shadowed head and body and bent arm with the paper glazed over in the dim light. The reddish earth floor.

"Johnson!" Millen demanded, voice hard and sharp. "Open the door!"

King lifted his left fist, hammered sideways on the door. Immediately a bullet hole erupted in the planks, and a crash inside of a rifle exploding.

Millen jerked erect from the window, wheeling, but it was King who staggered sideways away from the door. His rifle falling, his arms

clamping up around his chest, his face contorting in pain as he sprawled, then hunched together clutching himself.

Millen stared for an instant in shock at his partner jerking in the snow, then at the sudden, terrible hole torn out of the blank door he knew suddenly with such horrible, sickening clarity.

"Johnson, you bastard!"

And he hurled himself sideways, down towards King, the search warrant flying unnoticed from his hand. Immediately behind him the window shattered as the rifle inside the cabin crashed again.

Millen lay flat in the snow, King just ahead of him. The window was broken now and he had to—he raised his head slightly, back towards the river bank and saw Lang and Verville there, up on the bank now and sprinting apart towards bushes. He waved quickly, waiting for the sear of the bullet from the cabin behind him that he would never hear—you practised this, training, but you never thought it would actually happen, not really to you, a killer bullet from a wordless man—but nothing hit him, yet, and he half raised himself, waving furiously, heedlessly, and in an instant the thud of a bullet into the logs of the cabin and a crash—Verville, good, shoot, shoot!—and another from Lang, and the window smashed again. He hurled himself in a desperate low lunge through the snow towards King.

"Al... Al..." he was beside him, he had to get him out from under the cross-fire, "are you bad—" but King was breathing, unconscious but breathing, that was clear, jerking spastically into the snow but still breathing, that was all that mattered now though the snores of blood at his mouth and nose jolted Millen with fear and he heaved himself down to King's feet, got his mitts around them and started crawling for the corner of the cabin. And dragging King, their two bodies floundering slowly away in the snow from that smashed window, that blank lethal door.

Where the bullets thudded regularly now, and the rifle inside replied just as steadily.

The snow was desperately deep and brittle. It slipped like blood under Millen's churning knees and elbows and he could have screamed in rage at this clumsy, vicious slowness if he had had any breath, but he got King past the cabin corner and closer to the bank not knowing if he was killing him with this dreadful dragging, only knowing he had to get

him away, but then he could stop, gasping, and sit up. He got his bare
hand up into King's tight curl, up under his clamped arms. His hand
came away streaked with blood. Shot through the chest . . . sideways,
King had been standing sideways so in under the left arm, all the way
through the width of the chest, there was heart, lungs. . . .

Blood crusted around his nose but no new blood, amazingly, nose
or at his mouth. Millen looked up suddenly to the cabin. King's rifle and
the warrant lay in the snow in front of the pale door. It was
pock-marked with bullets now, the window smashed completely. And
the 30-30 barrel lunged out there at that moment, jerked as it fired.
Lang on the left over near the spruce dived behind a tree. Millen waved
furiously at him.

"Stay down, you guys," he hissed under his breath. "We've got
enough trouble here."

Verville was solid, straight ahead and shooting quick,
out-of-sequence shots. Exactly right. Then Lang waved from behind
his tree, took aim and fired. The bullet tore away something at the window frame: the 30-30 jerked out of sight.

"Johnson!" Millen roared, "I'll get you for this!"

A bullet smashed into Lang's tree.

Millen bent to King; it was impossible to carry him with the soft
snow on top and the breaking drifts underneath. He would have to drag
him to the near river bank.

And he did that, his breath sobbing in his chest, as gently as he
could slide King on his back and pulling on his bent-up legs. He got
him down, opened his clothing and felt for the place where the bullet
should have come out. There was not even a blood stain on his right
side; anywhere. It must have been the thick door.

"Okay, okay," he was muttering, "hang on, tough buddy and we'll
get you outta . . . we'll get you—"

King's eyes were open. Glazed in pain, blinking, unable to speak,
but he was certainly conscious. A good tough man, hard as a rock under
Millen's gentle fingers.

"Hey," he said, "hey my friend. Just lie still, don't move." He was
feeling along King's right side. "The bullet, I think, went right through
your chest. There's a bulge . . . I can feel it under your skin here, by these
ribs."

King flinched with pain.

"I'll leave it alone," Millen said, pulling King's clothes tight around him again. "And get you a slug of whisky."

A sound above them and Millen's head jerked up: it was Verville, sliding down the bank towards them. In the distance a Lee-Enfield fired, and the 30-30 barked in reply. Millen quickly spread his own parka over King on the snow and stood up to Verville.

"He's alive, okay," he said to the Metis trapper, "but the bullet's in him. His only chance is the doctor in Aklavik, how fast can we do it?"

"It's eighty miles," said Verville slowly. "That Husky River trail is rough, cliffs, up and down."

"And the dogs are tired already." Millen did not mention themselves, the men who had just run the forty-five miles from Fort McPherson. It was the dogs who would have to get them through. The men could force themselves, but the dogs would have to run until they died.

"We got three men, take turns breaking trail, then Knut's team, empty, then mine with him . . . well . . ." Verville said, still slowly, looking down into King's eyes momentarily open, but seeing the windswept cliffs of the Husky River trail north, up and down, and then the open tundra where the wind never stopped licking up the ground-drift.

"Twenty hours?" Millen said.

"Maybe . . . twenty-four," Verville answered.

"Get Knut, quick," Millen said, "and bring the sleds here."

He bent down to King, whose eyes were closed. Perhaps he was, mercifully, unconscious again.

*Part Three*

# The First Manhunt:
# Rivers and Wilderness

# 1

A TRIPLE SUN GLOWED on the southern horizon. You never see anything like that in Nova Scotia, thought Constable Paul Thompson as he came out of the rough log building that was RCMP Headquarters in Aklavik; and you'd never feel it this cold either—but he could have laughed. Sent straight to the Arctic on his first posting; he had no dream of anything better. It might have been Herschel Island and whalers from all over the world frozen in there, but last summer the police had moved headquarters here to Aklavik: the Place of the Brown Bear. A marsh and mud point where the Dene had camped for generations, sticking out into the western channel of the Mackenzie River Delta.

The rim of the thirty-minute winter sun emerged on the south horizon sometimes inside an enormous halo of smudged, flaming light; sometimes a cross stretched through and across the entire circle, or, like today, two brilliant repetitions of the sun itself stood one on either side of the bands of the cross with the air so cold it seemed to hang in silver crystals. Sun dogs. Sun tripled as if to make up a little for all the endless darkness. Thompson laughed, hauled in air laughing and it burned like ice in his chest. To resist the cold he could feel every muscle in his body, marvellously.

One by one the dogs below him to the sweep of the frozen Mackenzie began to howl. Three trapper teams in for trade were staked there among the widely chained town dogs. Usually that orchestration began in the darkness; one would start and soon they worked themselves up to full yodeling uproar. Now they were shaking their haunches out of the snow, nothing shining about them, huge bony brutes. He saw they were all lifting their snouts south, howling miserably. For a moment Thompson's eyes could find nothing on the white tundra stretching south. Only the Arctic sun, almost eerie, and certainly unnatural to him still, like a man with three heads—but a black dot was moving there. Squinting hard, he heard the distant crack of a rifle shot, followed by two others close together.

A dog team, and two, three men moving with it. Very slowly. He heard doors opening behind him, people coming out and shading their eyes south. Thompson wheeled, hurried back into the police building as the Inuit and Dene and English voices grew in the wide space that served Aklavik as street.

In a minute Inspector Alexander Eames came out into the sunlight with him. He lifted binoculars, adjusted them for a long moment south. "You're right, Thompson," he said, in his precise English way. "Get Dr. Urquhart."

The young constable ran off towards the Anglican Mission Hospital as Eames lowered his glasses and turned to the trappers who were gathering around him.

"It's police, bringing someone in," he said. "Only four dogs. They could use some help, I should think."

Lazarus Sittichinli, a Dene trapper, and several Metis men nodded and ran down the slope to their staked teams. More people of Aklavik were coming from their scattered log cabins, from their tents piled over with snow, and the huddle of igloos north and west of town. By the time the teams returned there were over a hundred men, women and children of half a dozen races clustered about in their heavy outdoor clothing, waiting to see what emergency was arriving from the barrenlands. They were people of the far north who all their lives lived within one simple accident of death, and they waited quietly, a community to help as it could or mourn if necessary.

Sittichinli's sled ran up first. He had simply cut the dogs off the sled coming in and loaded it bodily onto his own. Corporal Millen crouched on the sled, holding the other battered sled on as best he could; and there lay a man wrapped up and tied down in it. Motionless, only a bit of his face showing through the white rime of his parka: a trace of

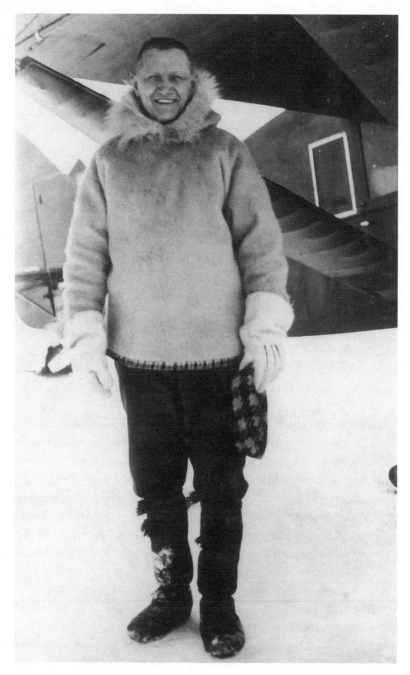

Alexander N. Eames, RCMP Commanding Officer, Akalvik

hoared breathing rising spasmodically. Some of the people crowding forward recognized Constable Alfred King of Fort McPherson.

Eames pushed through the crowd with Doctor Urquhart following. Millen looked up, his frost-hammered face totally exhausted.

"Hello Alex," he said to his superior officer.

"Spike, I . . . what happened to King?"

"He's still alive," Millen said, "more or less," and started to untie the wounded man. Immediately several men bent to help him.

"No, no," Urquhart said after one glance. "Don't take him off, just get him straight to the hospital."

Sittichinli nodded and shouted to his team. But the other team arrived just then with Lang and Verville aboard and their four exhausted dogs straggling loose behind; it was a hectic moment before Sittichinli could get moving in the surge of the crowd, but then all followed as both the sleds slid up the street. Millen started to run, still holding King on but there were many strong hands available now: he dropped back and strode beside Eames.

"We broke Lang's sled at the Big Bend of the Husky River," Millen said. "And two of his dogs and one of Verville's are dead."

"You cut the others loose?"

"Yeah. They should come in, maybe if—"

But just then a young man with a note pad and pencil in his bare hands bulldozed through the moving crowd around them.

"Inspector, Inspector Eames!" he gasped in the frigid air, already shivering in his light jacket. "Has a policeman been wounded? Was it a shoot-out? Where did—"

"Get some proper clothes on, Mr. Callaghan," Eames said roughly. "I'll explain whatever's necessary, later."

The young man stared at Millen an instant, then dashed ahead between people, trying to get a glimpse of King on the moving sled.

"What the hell is that?" Millen demanded.

"Mr. Morden Callaghan of the *Edmonton Journal*," said Eames with heavy sarcasm.

"A reporter?" Millen was incredulous.

"It's New Year's Eve tomorrow, and Edmonton wants to know how we northern savages celebrate up here."

Millen groaned with more than exhaustion.

"How did all this happen?" Eames said.

"Listen, Alex," Millen peered at him anxiously, voice low, "I think it was my fault. We went up the Rat River to check a complaint and I . . ."

"All right," Eames said quietly, "all right. We'll take care of King first."

Dr. Urquhart was trotting beside Sittichinli's sled. King's eyes were open now, and staring up blank with pain as the runners squealed, bounced on the rutted street.

"We'll have you in a bed in a minute," the doctor said bending down and brushing the ice from the wounded man's face. "Just a little bit and we'll have you in a nice warm hospital bed."

2

SPIKE MILLEN WAS DANCING. Lazily, the quiet violins of a gentle waltz soothing him into a dream of warmth and rest and the incomparable touch of a lovely woman in his arms, her blonde hair a drift of fragrance over his cheek.

". . . to sleep around the clock," he was murmuring into that soft blondness, "twice around, a long hot bath, steak and apple pie . . . and then dance out the old year with you . . . ahh . . ." he almost stretched luxuriously in the very movement of the waltz, his mind blank, blank, ". . . 'earth hath not anything to show more fair'. . ." he quoted dreamily, and sighed.

"I know, I know," Shirley Adams' voice had a thin strip of irony along its edge, quite out of keeping with the way she fit against his chest. "Heroes just misquote poetry, they never ache."

"Ache?" Millen tilted back and stared at her in astonishment. "Ache, after two short back-to-back hundred-mile patrols and a fast little 'shoot-out,' as they will say in the papers and then a twenty-hour run into Aklavik at forty-two below—ache?" His drawl pulling the word into two long syllables.

"Corporal Millen," she began in her most severe impossible-patient tone, "you are full of . . . statistics!"

And she burst out laughing, losing her rhythm with the music as his laughter caught hers. He stood back, bowed graciously.

"I am sorry, Nurse Shirley, my very dearest lady, I am truly sorry my conversation is, for this festive occasion so . . . so profoundly inadequate!"

She curtsied, raised her arms and they were waltzing again. Close.

"Indeed sir," she said against his ear. "Why Constable King flat on his back can converse circles around—"

"But his footwork, ma'am," he interrupted, "his footwork?"

"Will be better than ever, with a bullet snuggled between his ribs . . ."

She felt him tense in her arms and she went on quickly, trying to make amends.

"Dr. Urquhart says the thick door saved him, it slowed the bullet so much."

"It still tore a hole right through him," Millen said quietly.

"Oh, we sewed everything up so beautifully, and he's so strong, all that running behind sleds just like you, he'll die of nothing but old age."

"Won't that bullet there bother him."

"Not a bit," and she tilted back, smiled up into his face. "Imagine what a conversation piece, when he takes his shirt off!"

He smiled a little but his eyes were far away and abstracted; he had not heard her best sally.

"Who'd want to die of old age," he muttered.

A hand tapped his shoulder; he looked about, recognized it without looking at its owner and jerked himself back into the light banter of the New Year's Eve dance. "Behold, ma'am, the clammy hand of death. It is already upon me."

But Staff Sergeant Frank Hersey, in the full dress uniform of the Royal Canadian Corps of Signals, would not be deterred. He insisted, and Shirley laughed easily.

"I refuse," Millen said, dancing on. "You can dance with this beautiful woman every weekend, you Army guys sit in your warm Wireless Station all winter—"

"Hardly the hand of death," Hersey said grinning.

Millen stopped dancing suddenly and with his circled arms bent their three heads together. In the centre of Aklavik's year-end celebration, they were a small static island.

"Wouldn't you have to say, Shirley," he said very seriously, "that this Signal Corps uniform is downright deadly?"

"Catch up with the world, Millen." Hersey's voice had a thread of something beyond banter. "If you'd had us and one of our radios at that cabin, you could have brought in a doctor and all the reinforcements you need to get Johnson, without leaving him and—"

"Who needs an army to bring in one man?"

"Oh? Well," Hersey was almost drawling now, "I don't know, but I think your inspector has Riddell raising one right now, on our radio."

"What?" Millen stood stunned.

"He got us to set up in his office," Hersey continued, "and he's broadcasting all over the north for men he wants to come in and—"

But Millen had wheeled, his broad back was lurching between dancers, away swiftly. Hersey looked after him a moment in astonishment, then shrugged and turned to Shirley, his arms coming up in grinning invitation. She raised one eyebrow at him with no particular enthusiasm on her handsome face.

"You certainly do have a technique, sergeant," she said.

Hersey was very close to her. "You know me," he said. "I enjoy any challenge."

There was not the faintest memory of blonde hair and dark brown eyes in Millen's head as he strode through the frigid keening wind of the darkness towards Eames' office. The snow was trampled, ridged by sleds and feet, but he started to run. Down by the river flats, where Lindbergh had landed to refuel that summer, the huskies were howling like a requiem. Millen was almost sprinting when he reached the low police buildings and he burst in just as the other army signaller, Robert Riddell, whom he had once met at Arctic Red River, was signing off his message.

". . . Aklavik Headquarters, over and out."

The expression on Millen's face froze the army sergeant and the two junior police officers, Thompson and McDowell, where they stood beside the desk with its cumbersome radio and wires and batteries piled four high. But Millen looked only at Eames seated beside Riddell in front of the microphone, his long-nosed English face held in unrufflable calm. Which made Millen even angrier.

"I told you, Alex, I told you twice I made a mistake, how much clearer—"

"I'm just informing the trappers that Johnson has shot a—"

"You want to haul in everybody in the delta?"

"I'm not 'hauling in' anyone," Eames said, annoyed. "Now, can't we talk this over privately?" he gestured to the other men, staring.

"What does it matter, they know corporals blunder! Hell, in twelve years I've known inspectors and superintendents—" Millen caught himself. "Alex, I knew Johnson didn't like King and his way of treating people but I took Al there anyway and then I come back by the book with three men and a warrant, I should have—"

"You don't try to kill a man because you don't like him."

"I'm telling you, I know exactly what I did wrong! Don't make it even worse now by doing again what I did. I can talk him out of there."

"When you shoot a man through the chest," Eames said slowly in his clipped English voice, "you intend to kill him."

Millen burst out, "Johnson will not kill me!"

Eames stared at him, face expressionless.

"I was standing directly in front of his bare window, and he shot at King through the plank door!"

"So you're a witness; he's a criminal now."

Millen had to concede that. He wheeled, frustrated. "Well, okay, okay, but that just means he'll shoot even more desperately now."

"So, how can we get him out, without shooting?"

"Talk!"

"Of course we'll talk, if he does. I thought you said you tried. You think he'll talk more now than before he started shooting?"

Millen jabbed a finger at the radio, "I don't know—why don't you raise his cousin Erickson on that damn thing? Maybe he could help talk him down."

"I'm trying," Eames said. "But he's not near a radio, he's over the Richardson Mountains somewhere in the Yukon. It could take half the winter. Listen, I've contacted William Nerysoo, and you and I are going there with a show of force and we'll—"

"How many men?"

"At least eight, maybe—"

"A goddamn army!" Millen's face burst purple. "In the old days they needed one RCMP officer who knew his stuff and he'd ride into a whole camp of armed Sioux, alone! You know how many dogs you'll need just to haul dogfood in this weather for eight—"

There was a flurry of shooting outside, rifles cracking as dogs howled and then quickly shouts and cheers. Millen stared about for a moment, startled, but Eames looked at his wristwatch. Midnight, the first minute of January 1932.

"Spike," Eames said gently, "I know how many dogs it will take, but what's the alternative? It's a miracle he didn't kill King, and if you go in there alone now to talk and he shoots you too, how do I explain that? To anyone?"

Millen's big hands were clenching deep in his pockets; Thompson stared at him with frank, open admiration. The young constable had never accepted that the law was so unequivocal, could be so automatic in its application as the cut-and-dried police instructors in Regina had insisted, the law must be—

"Thompson," Eames ordered wearily, "finish typing the report for Superintendent Acland in Edmonton. McDowell, you're on supplies. Okay Riddell, thank you for setting up in here, saves a lot of running around."

"Any time, inspector," Riddell said, already packing his equipment, "any time we can help."

Millen had not moved. Thompson saw he was staring straight ahead at the Union Jack draped against the portrait of King George V, as if he were already running a sequence of moving pictures through his head—and not at all liking what he saw. Yes, Thompson thought, life and death confrontations must raise questions, they must, he thought even as he heard outside Aklavik's celebration of the New Year, families, friends, dancers, drunks, outroar the dogs' woeful chorus along the frozen river.

# 3

AT THE CABIN ON THE RAT RIVER only the sky flamed a shifting, dazzling celebration of northern lights into the new year. In the fierce, silver cold, smoke from the chimmney drifted over the snow roof, curled down past the dim light playing inside the canvas that now covered the smashed window. Nothing else moved in the frozen air.

Inside, light from spruce logs burning in the fireplace wavered about the small, cave-like room. A rifle leaned against the earthen wall at the head of the bedroll mound. A body lay there, curled on its side.

Albert Johnson's eyes were closed in deep sleep. But suddenly, without the slightest movement of his body, they were wide open. Staring straight ahead. Staring at the plank door so close to him in the tiny cabin, at the traverse log that barred it from inside; his eyes seemingly intense enough to see, between the nail-heads capped with thick hoarfrost, the bullet hole driven into the top of the middle plank.

# 4

As Edgar Millen knew from experience, Inspector Alexander N. Eames was nothing if not thorough in any preparations he made. Especially for a patrol that was to bring in a man who refused to talk to police, had clearly intended to kill one of them, and then kept an officer and two special constables at bay with pin-point rifle fire. So it was almost noon on Monday, January 4, 1932, before the posse could leave Aklavik.

Thirty-five dogs on five heavily loaded sleds with seven men cut through the low brush of the Mackenzie delta and out onto the tundra on the Husky River trail. Special Constable Lazarus Sittichinli led with his team from Aklavik, Millen taking turns with Eames riding and running. Constable McDowell had the RCMP Aklavik post team, and alternated with Thompson who was learning to drive, very quickly though the stubborn dogs made it seem long to the inexperienced Nova Scotian. Special Constables Knut Lang and Noel Verville—quite recovered with their teams, though Verville had added two dogs from his brother in Aklavik—completed the patrol. They were to meet William Nerysoo at the junction of the Rat and Longstick rivers.

There was a bad ground-drift when they left Aklavik, and a blizzard broke the first night of their camp, while they were still on the tundra. They could only dig in, wait. And wait. There was no snow falling; the wind gusted between thirty and forty miles per hour and drove the gravelly ground snow at them like knives, night and day. On the morn-

Leaving Aklavik on Johnson patrol, January 1932

ing of Thursday, January 7, the temperature was fifty-two below, Fahrenheit in a completely white, howling world.

The wind made for a total windchill equivalent of one hundred twenty below. Eames worked the mathematics of that out in his hammering double-walled tent, wrapped in his caribou sleeping bag and warming his fingers regularly around the Coleman lamp. What a damned report to make in his daily diary.

A white mound pushed into the tent, fumbling quickly to close the flap as the tearing wind bulged the tent out and almost knocked over the lamp. It was Millen. He shoved back his caribou hood and crawled forward to sit on his down bag. The small tent was packed tight with their bodies, breathing.

"Any sign of a break?" Eames asked needlessly.

Millen shook his head.

"The dog feed's just about finished," he said.

"I didn't order a five-day—" Eames began testily, then stopped. "Sorry."

"Once on a patrol to Holman Island," Millen was almost smiling in reminiscence, "Charlie Kalvak and I couldn't move for eight days. We played poker. I've still got the count on one of my report pads—3,678 games."

"He must have won two-years' salary off you."

"I wouldn't play him for money, hell, we played for icicles. The weather was so bad we couldn't build a new snow house and the one we were in was all dripping inside—Charlie had a pile of ice two feet high when the wind finally stopped."

Eames laughed aloud. "Piled up like wood, a stack of icicles in an igloo!"

"When this breaks," Millen said after they finished laughing, "you should send two teams back for more feed. We can't work without food very long in this kind of cold."

"You take the supplies, meet Nerysoo and go for Johnson alone?"

"Send whoever you want, but if he's stubborn and it takes a while to persuade him to come out . . ."

Millen's voice hung in the air. Despite their crowding, it was so cold inside the tent that even with the lamp and stove going their words drifted like white clumps of frost from their mouths.

"How far to the Rat River?"

"About four, five hours, when that stops."

They listened for a moment, as they had listened for three nights and two days; they could hear nothing different.

"Our supplies should stretch two days, don't you think?" Eames said finally.

"Probably."

"It'll break. It has to. And we'll get down there and persuade him fast."

"What if he's gone?" Millen said.

# 5

ON FRIDAY, JANUARY 8 the storm broke, and in the late-afternoon darkness the entire patrol reached the Rat River where William Nerysoo had camped through the blizzard alone, waiting for them. His supplies were lower than those of the police, so they made their plans around a quick sketch map the trapper drew, and by noon on Saturday Millen was up on the now-familiar bank peering through brush at Johnson's cabin. It was only forty-four below, and there was less snow; the wind had driven it down, hard and level all across the promontory.

A raven called raucously in the spruce and flew away. Calling.

Millen signalled behind him and with a soft crunch, a bit of slide, Eames' head came up beside him.

"He's still here," Millen said, puzzled. "There he is."

Across the clearing Johnson's short, broad figure stood at his woodpile. He turned to watch the raven fly away under the grey sky, looked

all around the trees, then abruptly he shifted his axe to his left hand and
bent, picked up his rifle in his right. He walked fast to the front of the
cabin, stepped down into the door-well, and disappeared.

"You thought he'd be gone?" Eames said.

"Yeah. And he's heard our men in the trees."

Eames was studying the clearing. "There's three feet of snow under
those spruce," he said finally. "And everything is . . . very close range.
The clearing's too small, really, little manoeuvrability."

"Alex," Millen said quietly. "Look, when he shot King, I'd have
gladly killed him—not make one sound, just shoot without warning—
but look at it from his point of view. He meets King twice, me once, we
don't know if he has anything to hide but he acts like he's mad at something, somebody. We know nothing except he calls himself Albert
Johnson. I never even got a next-of-kin from him down south if anything went wrong. So let me go alone now, and knock on the door."

"We've been over this," Eames said, clipped. "If he's heard us in the
brush, it's too late for that."

The inspector slid down the bank and signalled to his left; Noel
Verville was there, half hidden in brush. He returned Eames' signal and
turned and waved to someone further in the brush. Eames lifted his
parka and unholstered his revolver.

Millen came down the bank and picked up his rifle lying in the
snow. His face was set as if turned to ice in the stinging cold. The
Lee-Enfield was a wonderful weapon, so reliable you never had to worry
about it even at sixty below. He had shot seal, Dahl sheep, moose, more
caribou than he could count with this rifle. He levered its smooth bolt
once, and looked up stonily at Eames.

"You got your revolver," Eames said, "if we need it close in?"

"Yeah."

Eames nodded, stuck his revolver in his right parka pocket, and
then they both walked up the bank. Wide apart; and when they stood
on the river bank above the point where he and King had first camped,
it seemed to Millen, as he looked at the cabin blown over hard with
snow now, that he had already stood here half a lifetime, stood here or
imagined he had, he could not now quite tell which, and had had to
plough those thirty yards through snow—their old tracks were gone, the
wind had wiped the world clean and left not a faint shadow of his old

trail in the harder drifts—had he ever actually moved across—but of course he had, time and again and he knew there was something possibly lethal coiled in that small snow-covered bump ahead, waiting to explode. But he could not believe it, not yet because Johnson could not be a killer, he knew that though how could a man intend not to kill when firing at another through his door? He was not a killer, though how—

"Mr. Johnson!" Eames shouted beside him. "Mr. Johnson!"

Millen shook himself, and concentrated. On his right, behind spruce and well spaced, knelt Special Constables Lang and Sittichinli, their rifles ready. On the left, along the frosted brush of the river's edge Special Constables Nerysoo and Verville had their rifles up over the bank. And behind the cabin a bit to the right, Constables Thompson and McDowell stood, their rifles in front of them and waiting for the signal. To charge, if necessary. Boxed in, a show of force, inevitable force to scare him into surrender. What if he didn't scare, by force?

"Everybody's ready," Millen said without moving his head. He heard Eames take a deep breath.

"This is Inspector Eames, Royal Canadian Mounted Police, Aklavik Headquarters. Constable King is badly wounded, but alive. He is alive. We have you surrounded. Come out and give yourself up. Do you hear? Come out, give yourself up!"

Eames was gasping for breath from shouting in the ferocious cold. They waited, but there was no sound or movement at the cabin.

"Johnson!" Millen could not control himself, or the crack of strain in his voice. "This is Spike Millen. King is not dead. You're surrounded!" The air in his chest and throat was like knives, scraping him raw. "Surrender, Johnson, surrender!"

They waited, motionlessly frozen.

"It's tough . . ." Eames whispered suddenly, "hard to believe anyone's in there."

Millen was intent on the cabin. His breath sobbed slightly in his throat but he was suddenly feeling something he could not explain to himself, a weight like lead in his chest and the dead-blank window drew him. He was leaning forward in the intensity of his stare; it was not the window, Johnson would not use the window again, he was suddenly certain.

"Johnson!" Eames roared. "We're coming in to arrest you!"

And Eames pulled the revolver out of his parka pocket and stepped forward, lifting his left hand in the air as a signal. Immediately there was the thin whine of a bullet; Eames' parka fringe whipped about his thighs as a rifle crashed inside the cabin.

Eames dived into the snow and Millen on instinct finally dived down with him even as he comprehended there had been no rifle at the window. Another bullet whistled over them and Millen fired dead into the open window, there was nothing else to aim at, and another bullet answered him so quickly it seemed a reflex of his own. And so low he knew if he had looked up just then it would have blown his head apart. Where, low along the snow, the bullets were coming . . .

"Alex," he hissed, "are you—"

"Didn't touch me." Eames had his revolver up but did not shoot. He signalled quickly.

The trappers were firing steadily from their flanking positions. After a short barrage Eames signalled again; the firing stopped. Thompson and McDowell were lumbering forward through the deep snow towards the back of the low cabin. Millen shot carefully; his bullet hammered the door, and the rifle inside crashed again as a bullet thudded into a spruce tree, right. Thompson and McDowell had reached the cabin then, clambered up on the roof from the back, and immediately the trappers on both sides began firing again. There was a steady return from the cabin now and, strangely, it was regular out of both sides.

"How the hell's he doing that?" Eames gasped.

"He's down behind double logs," Millen said, aiming carefully, "and I think—yeah, he's cut rifle holes along the bottom . . . Thompson . . . Thompson . . ."

He was breathing that name against his rifle stock because the young constable was poised on the snow lip of the roof over the door; the trappers from the sides were keeping Johnson busy, thank god, but McDowell was there now too and then Thompson leaped down in front of the cabin, wheeled and battered at the door with his rifle butt as McDowell hunched down and shoved his rifle over the edge towards the gaping hole of the window.

"Thompson!" Millen roared. "The window!"

Thompson leaped into the door-well, he was prying, heaving at the unyielding door but then his head jerked up. The 30-30 barrel suddenly jabbed out of the window hole and Thompson hurled himself away, below it, his rifle flying as the 30-30 exploded. McDowell roared aloud, and fired straight down into the window.

Millen could not shoot: Thompson was flat, almost out of sight in the snow, motionless, and the trappers were shooting, furiously from the flanks. Johnson replied out of the cabin, first into the spruce, then towards the river bank; shooting so unbelievably fast there was no chance for a charge from either side even if they had planned it. McDowell leaped down into the snow beside Thompson.

Eames was swearing helplessly, not quite believing what was exploding in front of him. "He's like an army in there, I've never seen—"

Two mittened hands gestured out of the deep snow: the two policemen were crawling away from the door, waving.

"They're both," Millen gasped, caught his breath, "both okay!"

Eames was struggling with his other parka pocket; he tugged a Very pistol out.

"I won't . . . won't have them shot," he muttered, and fired the pistol into the air. Its flare settled over the clearing already grey in the quickly failing light.

Thompson and McDowell were past the corner of the cabin. Millen fired then, again into the open window though he knew now that he would hit nothing but some inside wall. Eames looked at him sideways in the snow, a kind of helpless disbelief still set on his cold face.

"Come on," he said.

And the inspector wormed around in the snow, began to crawl back. The trappers had stopped shooting on the Very signal, and Johnson had not replied to Millen's last shot. The time before he had at least reached the door, this time . . . and his mind convulsed suddenly in an abrupt fury. He heaved himself to his feet, faced the cabin fully erect for an instant, his rifle in his hand, and then he turned and walked towards the bank. Past Eames still lurching, hunching forward on his belly in the drifted snow.

"You idiot, get down!"

Millen plodded on. "I'm not crawling for him again."

Eames stared after him, then twisted to look at the cabin. It sat

there in the gathering darkness, the hard crust of its roof slightly trampled, but otherwise unperturbed by their assault. And silent. Eames
struggled clumsily erect, shaking his head, and trudged after Millen
down the river bank.

They lit flares around the edge of the clearing so that they could
keep watch on the cabin as the light disappeared. They were all very
cold as the excitement of the attack drained from them, and they built
three huge fires on crossed logs on the river ice to keep warm and cook
their last food. Thompson could not stand still even to warm himself;
he moved as lightly as if forty-below weather was meant for skinny-dip-
ping, though the rim of his parka was a complete circle of hoared
breath. In the glow of the cooking fire he showed Millen and Nerysoo
the stock of his rifle: the vicious groove torn there and the butt plate
sprung out in a jagged hole.

"Yeah," said Millen slowly. "Remember what a 30-30 can do."

"It just slammed, you know, right out of my hand," Thompson gestured with vivid excitement. "Like a club hit it."

Nerysoo said, stirring broth in an open pot, "On our side he was
shooting a Lee-Enfield."

"King's," Millen nodded. "He cut holes, loopholes on three sides
and had the Lee-Enfield sticking out one side and the .22 on the other."

"And the 30-30 everywhere else," Thompson said.

"He was real ready for us," Nerysoo said.

"That's what I can't figure," Millen said, "why'd he get ready like
that?"

"Like he knows exactly what we'll do," Nerysoo said so quietly that
Millen looked down at him crouched before the fire. The big Dene
stared wide eyed into the flames, abstracted, almost as if he were trying
to read something at the back of his own head.

Sittichinli dragged a bundle of wood between the fires, past Eames
and Lang unwrapping a package from the sled pulled in there. Millen
and Thompson came up to them: Eames was running his bare hand over
eight short slender columns of dynamite. And swearing under his breath.

"Frozen solid," he muttered. "Riddell said he'd really pack it so—"

Lang said, snapping a forked branch out of Sittichinli's bundle, "A
four-day blizzard's got no respect for nothing."

"Will it explode like that?" Thompson asked.

Lang shook his head. "It forms crystals inside, just go pfffft! We have to thaw it out."

Thompson's jaw fell. "How . . . how do you thaw . . . dynamite?"

Lang picked up the package and crunched to the farthest fire. "Like porcupines make love," he said cheerfully.

"Huh?"

Eames said, in his dry English accent, "Ver-r-ry carefully."

Thompson looked at him, a bit startled by the officer he had until now found only authoritative; but the dynamite intrigued him.

"Knowing how to do that should come in handy some time," he said, and followed Lang.

Millen stared into the leaping flames that Sittichinli now was stirring up with new brush.

"Alex," he said suddenly. Eames was repacking the sled. "How do you blow up a building without blowing up the guy inside?"

"He's fired at least fifty rounds at us. He has to take the consequences."

"Blast a guy apart for wounding a Mountie?"

"All right," Eames jerked to his feet abruptly. "I made my mistake too, I didn't count on a blizzard. But we don't have any time left for anything else."

Lang had tied the dynamite in the fork of the stick; he was turning it slowly from side to side in the unsteady heat of the fire. Thompson stood beside him, watching.

"I hope Knut knows what he's doing," Millen said.

"He was in the Big War, he knows."

Millen looked at his inspector silently. Above them on, the promontory McDowell and Verville kept watch on the cabin in the smoky red light of the flares; Eames finally faced Millen.

"Look Spike," he said slowly, "he planned, he got ready for us."

"Yeah . . . I know."

"That cabin is a fortress. And he's got ammunition, he can hold us off all winter. While we freeze."

"But you saw how he can shoot, and he didn't hit any of us. Why, huh?"

"You think he was shooting at Thompson's rifle stock?" Eames was incredulous.

"He could have . . ." Millen hesitated a moment. "But if he really had a record, he'd be over the mountains and heading for Alaska by now."

Eames shrugged. "I have to consider it an accident he hasn't hit us, after all that shooting," he said heavily. "We have to get him."

And Millen could not counter that. Why was Johnson still in the cabin? That was the key . . . and shooting to keep them at bay . . . those were the keys, the keys to something. 'I've been alone fifteen years,' he said at Fort McPherson loading his canoe. And 'people just get you in trouble'. What else had he said? Anything? Oh to be Sherlock Holmes in his smoking jacket.

Lang called, "Fifteen minutes, this'll be ready."

"Let's finish our hard-tack," Eames said, going to Nerysoo at the cooking fire.

The three flares at the corners of the clearing were guttering down to nothing when, with the others deployed around the edge of the clearing, Millen, Eames, Lang, and Nerysoo got into position under the spruce. The flares cast an eerie red glow over the trampled snow and the hump of the cabin, only twenty yards away. Lang pulled the four-pound bundle of dynamite from under his parka, where he had been keeping it warm against his body, and carefully wiped the long fuse clean.

"That snow is deep, it'll break," Eames peered through branches anxiously, the red light glinting on his sharp face. "Just throw it and get back."

"If it lands wrong," Lang said, "it just goes out."

"I don't want you blown up."

"I don't either," Lang chuckled. "You ready?"

Eames looked at his watch, and then at Millen. The corporal's face was set rigid, expressionlessly. In one hand he, like Eames, held his service revolver—and in the other a large flashlight. He snubbed it against his thigh, flicked the switch: it worked well, and he nodded to Eames. Who checked his watch again.

"They'll all be in position," he said. "Okay Bill?"

Nerysoo nodded; he was already crouched a short distance from them in the darkness below a spruce, his rifle up and ready. His round, dark face was set even more grimly than Millen's.

Lang turned at Eames' nod and in the shelter of his body he

Johnson's cabin after RCMP dynamite, January 9, 1932

snapped a match with his thumbnail. For a moment the flame would not catch on the fuse, then it flared up softly and Lang dropped the match, turned fast.

"Ten seconds," he said, and leaped into the clearing.

The snow broke under him badly, running, and in three strides he

was gasping in apprehension, the fuse burning down to the weight in his hand so fast like a sparkler, flashing. He was almost at the corner and he knew he had no chance to set it there, he could only throw it as he ploughed to a stop, trying to be careful but having to get rid of it fast and he had to wait an instant as it arched towards the window—would it?—and it thumped beside the space in the wall at a bad angle in the snow, but the flame was still bright and so close to the dynamite now he

could not breathe, he spun around and ran, carrying the memory of a
blurred white streak crossing inside the blackness of the window and
not thinking what it meant as he lurched back towards the spruce, desperately, and dived as he sensed the air suck in behind him and burst.
The cabin exploded spectacularly into the red darkness.

Through the blast and spray of snow and earth and splintered poles
and logs, in the quick flash of the dynamite's light Millen saw Albert
Johnson's cabin disintegrate. His mind was stunned in disgust, anger,
revulsion at having been brought to this, police work without reason,
only threat, sneaking surprise, violence, and his mind suddenly convulsed in blind fury and he leaped forward into the clearing, running.

"Spike!" Eames yelled, and blundered after him.

Millen charged past Lang. The logs were settling down, crashing
and groaning still into the rubble of their collapse and small flames ran
in bunches along their dry bark. Millen sprayed his light beam into the
mess of them, his revolver up, gasping, probing for whatever he did not
want to see, by god if he saw it he would—it was impossible, and then
he saw. He could not believe it even as it moved there in the black space
between logs and smoke and the small spurting flames.

It was the man's head. Rising as slowly as a spectre, deliberately up
out of the rubble, its face too black and singed for any expression except
the relentless set of its slit mouth and glaring eyes.

And the inevitable rifle was there too, its muzzle and barrel and
breech and stock emerging up out of the smoking darkness to lie against
the black cheek as if the force of that explosion had fused it there.

Millen stared past the rifle muzzle into those eyes, as they stared
past the revolver muzzle back into his. Motionless.

The noise of Eames' running lurched closer. And then the rifle in the
ruins flashed. Millen's flashlight burst into shards of light at its crash.

Millen hurled himself backwards, knocked Eames sprawling in
front of the cabin. Immediately bullets from the posse all around hammered into the tangled logs or whined over into the trees.

"Spike?" Eames whispered desperately, scrabbling low against him
in the snow. "Are you hit, Spike?"

"Not a scratch," Millen answered. Absurdly he felt like laughing, as
if a steel belt had burst off him and he was free, light as drifting ash over
fire. "Didn't touch me, he just didn't like my flashlight!"

Rifle fire from the destroyed cabin passed steadily in the darkness over their heads. The posse answered, shooting high; the clearing was too dark now for them to be sure of anything.

"Let's get out of here," Eames hissed, hunching around.

But Millen held him an instant, so close he could see the streaks of exhaustion across his inspector's eyes. "Thank God, Alex, you didn't kill him."

Eames blinked, grunted. "We may be sorry for that yet too," he said. And crawled away.

Lang was kneeling, shooting at the logs and their dying little fires when the two men got back into the spruce. But Nerysoo just stood in the darkness, his rifle hanging slack in his hand.

"You're wasting bullets," Eames muttered to Lang. "Stop."

He fired his Very pistol in the air. Its explosion fell like a small umbrella, streaked tracer's like a very tiny celebration from the grey sky over the destroyed cabin. The bombardment all around stopped.

"He's still alive?" Nerysoo said almost fearfully. "In there?"

"Alive and healthy," Millen answered, and he chuckled now, the strange exhilaration burning in him as it had in Thompson earlier. "Didn't you hear that 30-30 cracking?"

"Twenty-five years of duty," Eames shook his head in disbelief. "I've never met anyone like this."

"Let's rush the bastard," Lang growled.

"We'd get him now," Millen said, "sure, but he'll kill at least two of us."

"Yeah," Eames agreed. "And we can't wait him out . . . god . . . no, no, we're going back to Aklavik. Spike, you and Nerysoo get short supplies from McPherson and come back here fast."

"Right," Millen was enthusiastic. "Twenty-four hours and we'll be back."

Lang was cursing in Norwegian, absolutely disgusted, as Eames strode away. "That goddamn blizzard beat us," he muttered.

Millen laughed aloud. "How'd you like it, Knut, be so alone your only friend was the weather?"

But Lang refused to laugh; and so did Nerysoo. The Dene trapper stood motionless beside the spruce tree, staring at the mound of rubble in the dark clearing. Apprehension, almost fear, on his face.

# 6

Thanks to Morden Callaghan, accidentally present from the *Edmonton Journal,* the shooting of Constable Alfred King had become a newspaper and radio story of some interest on January 6. When, on January 13, the radio report came south that Albert Johnson had defied a large police posse and withstood a "regular siege," as the reporter had it, on the Rat River, the world suddenly wanted to hear more. King was alive and holding his own with the bullet in his chest; fine, now what was happening to the defiant trapper? The sputtering new phenomenon of radio repeated, elaborated his story in every newscast. Among the innumerable headlines of world newspapers—Drastic Cuts in Arms Urged; World Leaders Vow All-Out War on Depression; Woman Held in Stabbing; JAPAN SET TO INVADE CHINA—between the pictures of grey soup lines along city streets, of massed Asian soldiers marching, and of the tiny Duke of Windsor doffing his hat to cheering thousands from a luxurious railroad car, there now appeared the headlines: Police Lay Siege to Arctic Hut; Another Policeman Wounded; Trapper Refuses to be Enticed from Behind Barricade. There were, however, no pictures.

Eames was happy for at least that. But when he received the telegram from Superintendent Acland about the *Edmonton Journal* headline he roared with most un-English rage. MAD TRAPPER REPULSES POSSE. Across the front page in broad red, his superior told him.

The headline could glare at him, infuriate him every time it caught his eye, but Eames, now efficiently organizing a second, larger posse, could not know that it would be radio that spread his name around the world. Radios and tiny crystal sets speaking aloud in thousands of kitchens and living rooms where newspapers never came. In the worst depression winter so far, radio would explode this story for him. Radio speaking across the polished King Edward Hotel bar in Edmonton where northern men leaned, listening intently as they swallowed their drinks.

". . . but the police will continue their all-out efforts for a bloodless capture. Superintendent A.E. Acland, commanding G Division of the

RCMP in Edmonton, says he believes Johnson is preparing his dyna-mite-shattered cabin against a third attempt to dislodge . . ."

The door of the King Eddie opened and a young man bundled in a heavy coat and fur hat rushed in. He thrust aside his scarf, searched in the gloomy light among the men leaning on the bar. Faces moved in the crystal there, glass and bottle mirrors behind the bartender, and the newcomer strode rapidly between tables towards them.

"Wop . . . Wop, you seen the paper?"

He jerked a folded newspaper out of his overcoat pocket as a stocky, round-faced man in a leather jacket tilted to look at him, gestured with a glass of Scotch to the domed radio speaking from among the flanked bottles of the huge bar mirror, and turned again to listen.

". . . Police efforts have been badly hampered by temperatures rang-ing to fifty below and periodic blizzards raging across the roof of the world. But Inspector Alexander Eames has declared it is only a matter of time before his new posse of eleven men will bring the Mad Trapper to answer for his deeds.

"In other world news, a march by twenty thousand unemployed men on the—"

The bartender reached up and twisted the volume down.

"Who needs to know more about that?" he asked the world in gen-eral.

A lean businessman at the bar looked at him sourly.

"Yeah," he said. "And how far does a man have to go, to get away from snoopy police?"

"You never get away from anything," the grizzly-bearded man beside him said, his parka half draped off his shoulders. "There's always some bitching government thing following you."

"Wop, look here," the young man shook the stocky man's shoulder, offering the newspaper. MAD TRAPPER REPULSES POSSE, the *Bulletin's* headline blared. "I got this terrific idea, about the Mad Trapper, it's—"

"North of the Arctic Circle," the lean man insisted loudly. "A man wants to be alone, there's thousands and thousands of miles of bleeding empty tundra. But no! Oh no, not the police."

He drank deeply, and the stocky man, Wop, nodded while turning a little at the insistence of the newspaper under his nose.

Wilfred R. "Wop" May, pilot

"Snardon, I saw what you wrote there in the paper," Wop said, "and I've heard more on the radio. Look, I'm being followed too."

"You are?" Gary Snardon asked in astonishment, his fingers caught in unbuttoning his coat.

Wop leaned forward, his smooth oddly boyish face intense, his eyes scanning blackly upward past his eyebrows.

"Oh yeah," he nodded. "How'd you like it, to go down in World War history as Number Six, eh? Not even Four or Five, Six."

"Hey, Number Six is terrific," the reporter insisted, "to even be an Ace, that's really great, Wop, but—"

"That's what's following me." Wop would not be budged from his certain whiskey knowledge. He began the toll on his fingers. "First there's Billy Bishop, Royal Air Ace Supreme, seventy-two kills. Then second, Ray Collishaw, sixty-eight kills . . . and third, and fourth and fifth, and then me, Wilfrid Reid 'Wop' May, I'm . . ."

The inevitable fact May had faced so often; he drank deeply.

"Johnson probably lost his farm," the bartender said to the grizzlied man, "something like that in this goddamn depression."

"Sure," the lean man interrupted too loudly, "and I bet his wife and kids burned up in the farmhouse fire, I just bet, some son-of-a-bitching thing like that and the cops, they're after him now, they can't leave him alone, oh no."

"Gary," Wop May was now closely confidential, "Number Six never makes the history books. They always stop at the top Five."

"Ahhh, Wop, you'll be there, the books will be full of—"

"Oh, I'll be there," May said heavily. "For sure, because the Red Baron was chasing me when Roy Brown shot him down. That's why I'll be in the history books, von Richthofen with ninety kills was on my—"

"Wop, you were the decoy, everybody knows you—"

"Not everybody. They don't know my guns were jammed, do they know that? I was helpless, run, I had to, what else could I do and my Edmonton buddy Roy Brown goes down in the history books, and me? Yeah, I was too inexperienced, guns jammed from firing too long, so run, the books won't mention when Roy Brown ran, when Billy Bishop ran, but me, I'll—"

"Wop, the King himself gave you the Distinquished Flying Cross!"

Snardon clutched the pilot's shoulder. "My idea'll get you in the history books real big, again. The Mad Trapper!"

"Damn it!" The lean man was aiming an imaginary rifle the length of the gleaming bar. "To have a cop at the end of a 30-30, make you sing!"

May was ponderously looking out of the top of his eyes at Snardon.

# 7

ONE THOUSAND FIVE HUNDRED winter air miles north in Aklavik Inspector Eames finished reading the telegram from his superintendent.

". . . and it is bad strategy, leaving all publicity aside, to run out of supplies when you have your man cornered. I am sure you will try to prevent a repetition of that. Superintendent A.E. Acl—"

Eames hurled the telegram on his desk cluttered with trail equipment and papers, layers deep, as McDowell limped in.

"That reporter, Callaghan, is outside—"

"Get him in here," Eames snapped, red faced. "And those army signalmen, Riddell and Hersey too."

Eames scanned a hand-scrawled paper, and in a moment looked up at an apprehensive young Callaghan facing him.

"'A second policeman was wounded by the Mad Trapper of Rat River,'" Eames read, and threw the paper on his desk. "Rat River is correct, but every other fact in your very first sentence is wrong."

"Constable McDowell—" Callaghan gestured to the door, and Eames cut him off.

"McDowell sprained his leg very badly on the Husky River ice. He is not wounded. Now, I want you to have three facts very clear or you will not receive another word of information on this case. One: we have no evidence that Johnson has trapped anything. Two: we have every evidence that he is not mad. He—"

"When he shot King," Callaghan hastily justified himself, "it sounded a lot like he was bushed, not saying a word and not coming out—"

"We have every evidence now," Eames continued relentlessly, "that he is an extremely shrewd, organized and resolute man, capable of quick action and reaction. Three: I will not have it broadcast outside that the RCMP are hounding some poor demented character out of his lonely cabin into the Arctic winter!"

There was a pause.

"Now," Eames said, "I want you to correct that story."

"I . . . I don't know, sir," Callaghan hesitated. "There's such unbelievable interest, all over the world, the radio picks up everything I write, there's—"

Hersey poked his head in the door; Riddell was behind him.

"Come in, come in," Eames said, and looked back once to Callaghan. "Then you correct the radio too."

The two army signalmen entered carrying the various parts of a large two-way radio set between them. They heaved them up on the desk. Callaghan had turned to go but stopped now, unable to leave for curiosity; then he caught the inspector's glance and walked out hastily.

"We've got the problem licked, sir," Hersey was enthusiastic. "This is a complete two-way radio, radius of up to a hundred and fifty miles, depending on atmospheric conditions. The cold won't touch it."

Eames was worried. "That's about half a sled load right there."

"Right!" said Hersey very cheerfully, misunderstanding. "And with the batteries we can get everything, the whole works on one load."

"The only real problem," Riddell said slowly, "will be to keep the batteries from freezing. On the trail."

# 8

IN HIS EDMONTON OFFICE, RCMP Superintendent A.E. Acland was facing another problem of modern technology. He was studying Captain W.R. "Wop" May in his fur flying parka, *Edmonton Bulletin* reporter Gary Snardon, notebook and pencil in hand, watching silently in the background.

"You are quite right, Captain May," Acland said at last, very carefully. "It would be the first time in history that a police force had used an airplane to bring a fugitive to justice, true, but—"

"Sir," May interrupted before the "but" could be irrevocably elaborated, "you know my record, I flew that rescue medicine to Fort Vermilion, the oil equipment to Norman Wells, and the mail now pretty regular to Aklavik, and I—"

"I read the papers too!" Acland smiled. "And our new Commissioner, Major-General MacBrien, is more than ready to use any modern means so we can apprehend criminals, he's sent us memos to that effect, but—"

"I've flown all over that country," May sat coiled forward with intensity, "in winter it's like the ass end of the moon. When they're travelling good and there's no blizzard it takes two days to get to Johnson's cabin. And most of that mushing in the dark. I can get there from Aklavik in thirty minutes."

"Of course you could," Acland said steadily. "But we do not drop bombs on fugitives. We bring them to trial."

"Have you got any idea what the darkness and the weather in that—" May interrupted himself, on the very edge of his chair. "Look, you want him to kill a few people first?"

"Captain May," Acland looked him straight in the eye, "we are not at war."

"Sir, I know war," May said, hard. "But it's the dead of winter, and your men need supplies. I can get them to them, fast."

"Nor," said Acland could turn his controlled rage on Snardon, "are we on record. Good day, gentlemen."

# 9

RCMP Corporal Edgar Millen and his men were totally unaware that the world clamoured to hear more about the trapper and his one-time fortress on the Rat River. After being hung up at Fort McPherson by another blizzard, it was in the brief hard sunlight of noon on January 14 that he finally stuck his snowshoes upright in front of the ruins of the cabin. The pale plank door had been shredded. He contemplated the burst splinters of it, then climbed over among the logs, looking for what he could see. Which wasn't much. He found the

Lee-Enfield, its breech smashed, and then peering under a split timber beside the remains of the fireplace he discovered the tunnel.

He bent low and peered in. Could a body . . . there were mounds, sacks perhaps in the far corners, and he crawled into the black cold, the tunnel echoing as his clothes scraped against the permafrost; long and deep enough to shelter at least three men. But there were only sacks: flour, rice, half-opened beans, what he had seen Johnson load into his canoe last autumn, an unbelievable time ago. And not a single fur, or bullet.

For a moment on his knees inside the dark earth there he forgot all the effort, the trouble Johnson had caused them in the ferocious cold. The smell of flour and soil; a man had dug his home here, built it well down into the earth and above it and been warm and sheltered; he had defended it and it had been blown up suddenly, but it had protected him even against four pounds of dynamite. He felt close to Johnson, who had laboured long to carve this out, the closeness of privacy and dark. If he stayed here, and thought, he would gradually understand. He was certain of it, very suddenly. And leaned against the wall, certain and waiting.

But after a moment he had to laugh to himself. Backed out, back under the split timber against the crude stone fireplace, where as he turned around on his hands and knees he saw a scrap of paper in the ashes.

A scorched corner of a picture: black and white snapshot badly browned but there were flowers on it, almost like a mass of flowers in a garden perhaps. Where you would expect a woman to stand, smiling, a memory to study between your fingers, for years. As these men in the north sometimes did with no sense of time outside. Or human change. The Arctic was like that, he knew, even for himself, time no rush here like outside, changing. Slowly Millen drew off his mittens and sifted through the ashes. Carefully, his fingers quickly stinging with cold, but scratching through every bit. There was nothing more, only this small brown edge of a picture gone in smoke.

"Spike," Nerysoo called.

Millen looked up between the jumbled timbers.

"His canoe is in the trees. And a meat cache, front quarter of a moose."

Millen got to his feet and put the scrap in his pocket. He gestured at the black tunnel opening.

"That's why our dynamite didn't knock him out," he said. "He dived in there."

"Ahh . . ." was all Nerysoo said.

Millen climbed up; over the clearing the wind was beginning to moan. He showed Nerysoo the smashed rifle.

"King's. He had no more bullets for it. Any tracks?"

"The wind took everything."

Millen stepped into his snowshoes. "So which way did he go?"

Nerysoo said, oddly, "He doesn't even have a dog,"

They began walking to the river bank where their teams waited.

"Everything he has, he takes on his back," Millen said, remembering that immense tumpline load at Fort McPherson. "And that's plenty."

"Alone," Nerysoo said. "He just goes away . . . to get away."

"Right. Upriver, towards the mountains."

"Alone all winter."

"Yeah," Millen said, not catching his tone. . "We better leave a message here for Eames. And all his many men."

He looked around the clearing once more. It seemed a shame to leave, it was all so familiar. Especially the door with the bullet hole; broken now, and which he had never seen open.

# 10

WHEN EAMES WITH HIS ELEVEN MEN found Millen and Nerysoo on January 17, they were systematically searching a short tributary of the Rat River. They had found Johnson's tracks in seven different places in seven different ravines, but it was the time for blizzards, for terrible cold and ground-drift even on the calmest of the very short days, and finding a man in that wilderness who did not want to be found was, in a sense, impossible. While the new men set up their camp, Millen led Eames up a height of land to show him. Up there just enough light remained to see distance.

"You're sure," Eames panted, slogging upward after Millen's long strides, "they're his tracks?"

"No question," Millen stopped then, his week-old whiskers hoared in the tremendous cold; he looked very tough, weathered, and strangely content Eames thought, plodding up. "He's made his own shoes, the pattern can't be disguised."

The tundra lay open before them in one giant sweep towards the Richardson Mountains, absolutely snow jagged and beautiful, a long line of broad teeth filed sharp and still touched by light on the horizon. The two men rested, breathing very carefully.

"He doesn't have to go there," Millen said at last. "Look."

He pointed left, parallel to the mountains. Out of sight into the coming darkness stretched the high, wind-swept plateau cut down by innumerable ravines filled with brush and stunted trees. A measureless landscape eroded like badlands, deep enough to lose cities, ripped, cratered, abused by unbelievable cold.

"Dear god," was all Eames could say.

Millen turned out of the wind, rubbing the frost off his whiskers. "When Johnson has to move," he said, "he walks up on the plateau. The wind wipes his tracks out in two minutes."

"Otherwise, he stays in the shelter of those canyons?"

Millen nodded. "We'll have to search them all."

Eames swore a long white cloud into the fading light.

"He makes some of those tracks to fool us," Millen said, "In fact, I think he watched Bill and me at least once, looking for him."

"What do you mean, he's not trying to get away?"

"I . . . I don't know. I haven't figured that out yet. But I will," Millen said thoughtfully, and turned, plodding back. Eames followed heavily.

"What's bothering Bill Nerysoo?" Eames asked when they neared the bottom of the ravine and could see the campfires leaping between the brush, the grey flanks of tents against the steel of the towering frozen cliffs.

Millen shook his head, trudging on steadily. "I don't think it's just him," he answered. "It's all the Indians."

"They're our best trackers," Eames said. "This is their country."

Millen said, "Bill's been very quiet since we blew up the cabin."

"We've got to keep them," Eames said.

Millen stopped, breathing easily in the cold, and Eames came panting up.

"Ever heard of the nana'?ih?" Millen asked.

"What's that?"

"A bad, angry spirit. The Indians think it sometimes takes people over,
can turn them into 'bushmen', we'd say . . . even make them unkillable."

Eames looked at him steadily, exhausted.

"We've got to keep the Indians with us," he said again, finally.

# 11

So THEY HUNTED. In the brief hours of the sometimes howling daylight,
the temperatures at best twenty-five below, at worst fifty-five. Each ravine
and creek, carefully, always at least two men together in case Johnson
decided at some point to stop moving ahead of them, to stop making the
tracks they found in short bits almost everywhere. Patternless as to his
movement. One of their men burned his hand, another's leg was slashed
badly getting two tangled teams apart; once they spent an entire day
searching down a long canyon because they discovered what seemed fresh
Johnson tracks coming off the bare tundra down into it. All the men, three
on either bank along the top, and Millen, Nerysoo and Sittichinli down in
the twisting canyon where any corner, any bristle of creek-piled brush
might suddenly explode with 30-30 bullets. Once a tree beside Millen
burst open in the cold like a rifle crack and he leaped crazily, certain he was
shot, and when they finally climbed up the cliff where Johnson had
climbed out Millen slipped, fell, and Nerysoo barely caught and anchored
him on a rock until Sittichinli reached them and hauled them both away
from an eighty-foot drop. They were tracking an indomitable ghost which
moved as if weather did not exist and laid tracks in whatever deadly spot
it pleased, up cliffs and over ice-skimmed running water that could catch
you with one snap of its innocent deadly surface.

"I see his big snowshoe tracks," Nerysoo said without a grin, "and
sometimes it looks like 'Bigfoot.'"

They were eating enormous supplies, their fifty dogs ravenous in
the dead-of-winter cold, and every night the signalmen worked desper-

ately on their radio. Trying to raise their buddies standing by in the signals building at Aklavik.

"We can receive okay," Riddell explained to Eames. "Aklavik comes in pretty clear, it's just we can't transmit. The battery's half frozen."

Hersey whipped off his earphones, staring at the pad he had been scribbling on. "Listen," he yelped, "this is crazy! Johnson is a world news sensation!"

"What're they saying?" Eames asked wearily.

"It's the radio news mostly; 'Gunfight at the top of the world'. . . 'Bloody battle looms' . . . and letters to editors, 'Stop hounding the poor Mad Trapper, leave him alone' . . . 'there's enough government interference in everything.' . . ."

Eames swore in disgust and pulled up his hood, turning to leave the tent.

"Hey, and 'Wop' May," Hersey went on, oblivious, "that air ace from Edmonton, wants to fly up here, and bomb Johnson out of his lair!"

"He'd have to find it first," Eames muttered, crawling out into the darkness.

Since there was no way of sending a message to Aklavik, he and Millen decided they would have to split the party and send at least three teams back for more supplies. But on the morning of January 23 they found Johnson's huge, indelible tracks again.

His snowshoe prints walked right through the middle of their base camp on the Barrier River. Between the tethered dogs, down one bank and up the other.

Millen came back into camp after following the tracks up to the wind-cleared tundra and found four of the five Dene men harnessing their teams. Nerysoo's sled was packed and ready for the trail.

"Bill," he said then.

Nerysoo looked up from the dog harness he was rubbing soft between his big mitts. His round, usually pleasant face so much harder than any cold could make it; he answered nothing.

"If Johnson's that close," Millen said, "then we really need your help right now."

Nerysoo worked on the harness. "Those are his big tracks," he said.

"Yes . . . yes, but we're tired out at night, maybe the dogs barked and we didn't hear them."

"No dog barked," Nerysoo knelt, slipped the harness over his lead dog's eager head. "We pushed him too hard, he's really mad at us now."

"We have to take our families in," Peter Snowshoe said. "It's too dangerous, leave them out here on the traplines."

"Okay, he's dangerous, but then we have to get him for sure."

Nerysoo finished with his dog, straightened up and came close to Millen. He ran his coiled whip through his hand, studying it carefully.

"Nobody chases a *nana'?ih*," he said.

"Bill, Johnson's just a poor bug—"

"A bushman, and I think he's really mad at People." The big Dene smiled a little, almost self-consciously. "Our People die, we're not scared to that . . . but a *nana'?ih* has too much power, it can kill you real bad. We leave it alone."

"Listen," Millen said fiercely, "you saw Johnson on that raft, you talked to him at his cabin. He's a human being!"

"He was," Nerysoo said. "Then. You blew him up and he isn't dead, he walks through here and fifty dogs don't smell or hear him."

"He's just taunting us, he knows we . . ."

"Yeah," Nerysoo was staring at the cliffs, "that's what they do. I never thought a white would . . . be careful, now it's white it could get you too."

"He shot King," Millen said, hard. "He has to be brought in, punished."

"He is punished. He's always alone."

Millen turned to Stittichinli, standing there, listening. "Well, Lazarus?"

"I give the inspector my word," Sittichinli said, almost sadly.

Nerysoo nodded and turned to his team. "Get up, dogs," was all he said.

Eames came up as Millen and Sittichinli stood motionless between the black heaps of their campfires, watching the teams run northeast at the bend of the Barrier River.

"Down to six men, four teams . . . and the radio's out," Eames said. "There's nothing to do now, but get back to Aklavik."

Millen slowly rubbed his frost-blackened cheek. A strangely hollow silence lay over the camp with the sounds of the Dene fading away. He looked along the river cliffs: was Johnson up there, somewhere, laughing? Did he ever laugh? He should be, now; he had gotten rid of all but one of their best trackers.

Lazarus Sittichinli, Dene tracker

Millen turned wearily to Eames, shaking his head. "Better take Hersey and his useless radio along too."

"Listen, Spike, there's the bush pilot in Edmonton that wants to come up here."

"To do what?"

Paul Thompson was coming towards them but the two officers were too intent upon themselves to hear the crunch of his feet.

"He could fly in supplies," Eames said, "easy, two, three trips a day."

Millen nodded. "And you'd get fifty men to sweep these ravines."

"We could get this damn business finished."

"You feel the whole world watching you?"

Eames exploded. "You've been after Johnson a whole month!"

"We're getting a bit more daylight every day."

"You want to chase him till summer?"

"An army won't find him," Millen said quietly. "He'd pick it off, man by man."

Eames glared at him, pointedly ignoring Sittichinli. "That 'bushman' stuff getting to you too?" he growled at last.

It was Millen's turn to explode. "He's bush smart, Alex, he . . ." he saw Thompson standing there then, watching them with his intense young eyes, and he controlled himself. "Listen, I don't know, if I did I'd have done it already. I . . . look, just give me Lazarus and two other men and keep us supplied. We don't need radios, planes—all this . . . machinery. This is country for men and dogs, those . . . mechanics have to burn down half the country to warm up their batteries!"

Eames looked at him steadily, said nothing.

"And you get a plane up here," Millen finished, "hell, they'll have to drain the oil every minute it's not running, they'll have to burn down the rest of the country trying to keep it warm."

Eames said, "You want an old western shoot-out, eh, man to man?"

"I don't want to push Johnson into killing somebody!"

"Then you should have told him long ago before he shot King!"

They were facing each other almost nose to nose. Suddenly Eames saw Thompson beyond Millen's shoulder, and they broke apart.

"Sorry," Eames said, glaring at the white river.

Millen had seen his look shift; and recovered himself. "He has to give himself away eventually, just to shoot meat," he said more quietly. "I've got this . . . feeling . . . something . . ."

"Okay. I need Lazarus to get me to Aklavik, but you've got your three men: Thompson and Lang and Riddell. Hersey comes with me."

"All right."

Eames turned towards the tents. "We'll leave as soon as we can get ready."

"Alex," Millen said after him.

"What?"

"Try to resist that plane, eh?"

Eames was going. "I'll do what I can."

Millen grinned suddenly at Thompson, standing silent so long he might have been frozen; but his face was eager, almost happy.

"You'll have to work now," Millen said. "This is a new patrol altogether."

# 12

"Spike. Spike!"

"Wha . . . what the—"

"Spike, it's just about seven o'clock!"

Millen's nose and one eye emerged out of his eiderdown bag into the yellow beam of a flashlight.

"Paul . . . hey, it's calm outside? No wind?"

"Forty-two below, and no wind."

"Real good. We're taking the day off." And Millen hunched back down out of sight.

Thompson's expression could not quite believe him.

"It's Sunday," Millen muttered inside his sleeping bag. "Go back to sleep."

"But . . ." Thompson was now totally confused. "No wind . . . it's great tracking weather!"

Millen's bleary eye glinted at him for a minute. "So? We'll let him make some tracks."

Thompson's flashlight clicked off and slowly his body rustled down into his bag. There was a stiff stillness; outside a dog stirred his chain.

"Anyhow," Millen said suddenly into the darkness, "don't you know Sunday is for pondering your spiritual condition?"

Thompson's response, when it came, was dry and edged. "Inspector Eames never mentioned that. He just asked me about my feet."

Millen snorted easily; irony, on a long patrol, great. He chuckled aloud, already feeling better for having been awakened out of heavy sleep. His right shoulder ached anyway, lying too long in one position on the packed spruce.

"The Indian trackers' feet were just fine," he said. "Their spirits weren't."

"They never told us about that in Regina."

"Oh, those strait-laced nits," Millen hunched over. "They just think 'the majesty of the law,' 'the honour of the force,' that's enough. Sometimes it is, but not all winter on the tundra in the dark, and never on a patrol like this. That's one sure thing those trappers that used to come into Edmonton and drink at the King Eddy taught me. They'd be in from the north once every two years or so and drink and talk, that's all they'd do, always at the King Eddy."

Thompson sat up. "And you'd go there and listen to them tell stories?"

"Yeah, that's when I first wanted to come north. I was in tech school then, and I'd sneak in there and listen to those old guys, Rags Williams, Carl Murdoff, George . . . all great guys with lots of fur money to drink and talk for months. It was John Bowen always said, 'To live alone you must have a clean spirit. That's the whole situation, a clean spirit.' So I asked him about that one day and he said living alone in the Arctic and not seeing another person for maybe five, six months was sort of like living in a dream, or waking in the middle of the night: you're inside yourself all the time and if you wake up with some worry on your mind there's nothing you can do about it then but worry some more, so it just gets worse and worse. That's exactly like living in the Arctic: you can't do anything about people outside from up here, and if it keeps nagging you it will just get bigger."

"Six months bigger?" Thompson said.

"Yeah," Millen said thoughtfully. "It can wipe you out."

"I've got nothing like that on my mind," Thompson offered into the frigid tent.

"Not even a girl pining away, waiting somewhere in Nova Scotia?"

"Naw," Thompson drawled, "there's plenty of time for that."

"There's one terrific girl in Edmonton," Millen chuckled a little. "But I'm not worried about her."

"How come?"

"She's not waiting."

Thompson laughed. "All I want," he said, "is to get back on Johnson's trail."

"Tomorrow," Millen said. "Today you just rest your nice clean spirit."

# 13

BUT IT WAS LATE ON THURSDAY, JANUARY 28 before they found the substantial tracks they needed so they could follow in the semidarkness. They were up a small tributary of the Barrier River by then, deep in the foothills of the Richardson Mountains, and a blizzard had nailed them down all day Wednesday. They followed the fresh snowshoe trail along the creek until they reached a point where another frozen stream entered sharply from the right: and there the track divided. One track went right, one left, and they disappeared around bends in two different directions. The dogs sank down, exhausted, and Knut Lang knelt where the tracks separated.

"How . . ." Thompson hesitated, "how could he go two ways at once?"

"Maybe like a damn Indian bushman," Riddell muttered.

"It's the same shoes," Lang said, almost apprehensive.

Millen said quickly, "We just divide, that's all."

Lang looked at the sky above the brush-tangled cliffs. "Not much light left."

"Okay," Millen said. "We'll stake the dogs here and you and Paul go right, Bob and I'll go left. If you find nothing in twenty minutes, turn around and we'll meet back here."

Lang and Riddell went to stake the dogs against the willows. Thompson stood staring from one track to the other.

Millen laughed. "There's not two of him," he said.

So they advanced, two and two along the tracks that might have been shadows of each other leading into the two gloomy creek beds before them. Thompson and Lang kept separated, close to the opposite banks though the trail they were following went up the middle of the

Snowshoes made by Albert Johnson

ice as openly as any trapper walking his trap line. The brush on the banks was open, then tangled, and after a few minutes the creek widened badly. They kept their rifles at the ready; there was no sound other than the soft swish of their snowshoes in the soft snow. They trudged on.

Abruptly around a curve the creek bent sharp left, away from a high cut bank. Here tall brush and deadfall was piled black in the middle of the creek bed and Thompson, approaching that, hesitated. The tracks swung in towards his side, close, and he looked around: across the creek Lang had noticed his hesitation and stopped to watch him. And then in the silence of his standing still, suddenly Thompson tensed, leaned forward to listen.

Thompson gestured: around the brush.

Lang came to him swiftly, walking so carefully now that Thompson himself could not hear him. They listened together at the tangle of logs: something was moving there, certainly something.

They looked at each other, quickly, and then muffled their rifles against their parkas as they cocked them. Thompson gestured at the trapper to stay, cover him, and then listened again. He took several careful steps forward, but could see nothing. Or hear it now.

And suddenly, a crunch of snowshoes. Thompson shouted, "Johnson! Albert Johnson! This is the police, come out!"

Silence, then quick movement: a figure in the gloom, obviously a man, obviously holding a rifle.

Thompson aimed, shouted, "Stop! Drop your gun or I'll—"

"Hey . . . hey . . ."

"Drop it or I'll shoot!" Thompson shouted.

"Hold it!" Lang barked behind him just as the distant voice called again:

". . . Paul . . . Paul, it's Spike . . . Paul!"

And so it was. Millen, with Riddell close behind him. Thompson dropped his rifle in consternation as Millen trotted close.

"Do I look that much like Johnson?" he grinned.

Thompson was shaking suddenly. "The . . . dark . . . I almost shot . . ."

"Good thing Mounties never shoot first," Millen said easily.

"I don't think I'd want to take you two guys on," Riddell said unsteadily, "alone."

Lang was shaking his heavy head in anger. "It's too dangerous, tracking separate in the dark."

"Yes," Millen agreed. "Let's get back and make camp." He put his arm around Thompson's shoulder and turned him around. "It's okay, okay. You know how Johnson did it? He starts up one branch of the creek, then walks backwards in his own tracks and lays another trail up the other—"

"One way, he's stepping backwards exactly in his own tracks?"

"Yeah. The tracks we were following ended just beyond that brush, these two creeks are really the same one."

"A real devil," Thompson muttered. They were all four trudging down the creek together, their rifles in the crooks of their arms.

Riddell said, "Breaking two trails is terrible work . . . why'd he do it?"

"Maybe so we kill each other," Lang said gloomily.

"Go on, Knut," Millen said, and chuckled. "He's just a joker. He's sitting on the cliff up there right now, watching us and laughing."

"He's really funny." Thompson had such disgust in his voice the other three men laughed aloud.

Soon Thompson joined them; their voices rang hard together along the cliffs of the nameless frozen creek.

# 14

THE SOLITARY MAN they were tracking did not hear their comradely laughter. After laying his double maze to entangle his pursuers as it could, he had continued up the creek two miles and then turned, climbed to the wind-swept tundra and crossed deliberately into the wind from the Barrier to the Bear Creek complex of streams. He had been here two days earlier, weathered a blizzard and now he found a rabbit in one of the snares he had set then. He settled in his camp under a bank overhang; while the rabbit legs roasted on a stick he set his rifle upright against his huge pack tilted against the bank and removed the snare carefully from the rabbit's neck. Shaking from hunger.

Once he had returned to his destroyed cabin on the Rat River, but the police had hauled away his supplies; and they had two men guarding his cache of moose meat. He had almost stepped on one sleeping under the spruce.

While the legs roasted over his tiny fire he checked first one hand, then the other for frostbite. He huddled towards the fire's small warmth, gaunt and trail worn, his woollen underwear and shirt, and even his leather outer parka and pants heavy with sweat and dirt and smoke and freezing. The cold crept at him around the base of the cliff.

He untied his pack, alternating hands to keep one warm in his mittens. He spread a small piece of moose hide on the snow and laid out his supplies in their usual neat pattern. He nudged the spit over the fire, then took a tiny package of salt from its place and sprinkled a bit over the roasted side. He replaced the salt and took the spit stick in his mittened hand and began to eat voraciously.

When he was down to raw meat he re-set the spit over the fire. There was a kind of quietness in him then; his hands no longer shook and it seemed now they could gain enough warmth from the fire even when he allowed himself to lean back, relax momentarily against his pack and rifle. But the rifle was so much part of him that when he felt it against his shoulder he shifted immediately, took it up and held it to the low flames. It was worn brilliant from being constantly in his hand, on his shoulder; the wooden butt shone like the inside of a worn palm, the yellow brass breeching and the blue steel of the trigger guard and long barrel, delicate as a stem pointing wherever he looked, the whole lay warm and lethal in his black, clawed hands, a numinous thing.

In the past three weeks he had been moving so close to his pursuit that he had not fired it once; not since he shot Millen's flashlight out of his hand.

He aimed the rifle directly into the fire, concentrated, and suddenly his finger tightened. Nothing happened: he had not cocked it. He lowered the rifle, laid it gently across his lap. He was studying the roasting meat.

After a time, however, his hand went inside his clothes and he pulled out two pictures. He glanced quickly at the top one: the two men and the fishing boat, but then he shuffled that under the other. The head-and-shoulders snapshot of a young woman in a low-cut dress, pleasant, half smiling, nothing obviously distinguishing about her; the unclear grain of black and white making it impossible to see any character in her eye and rather thin mouth with its slightly uneven teeth barely showing, or any distinctive swell of bosom. The man stared at it, and stared; the smell of roasting meat rose and he shifted the spit slightly out of the fire, still studying the picture.

"If you trust . . ." he began under his breath in singsong, "You'll be sorry, you'll be sorry in the end. There's someone out to get you . . ."

He moved the pictures: the boat and the two men side by side with the young woman.

"There's someone out to hurt you, there's someone out . . ."

Abruptly he shuddered, and a rage seemed to explode inside him. He dropped the woman's picture and tore a third of the boat picture away with his black, hard hands, directly through the body of the older man. He crushed that piece and threw it into the fire. Then he tore the other third of the boat off and threw it into the fire also.

He was holding the ragged strip of the young man, waving happily, hanging aslant from the mast of the boat. After a long moment he thrust that into the flames; he watched the grainy shadow of the young man bulge brown, catch, burst brightly into indistinguishable light.

Where the spears of heat from the tiny fire had melted the snow into pointed crystals, the picture of the young woman in her scanty dress lay, pleasantly non-committal, half smiling.

# 15

BY SIX O'CLOCK the four pursuers were awake; they had eaten and broken camp in the darkness by eight and when the long blue shadow that precedes the glimmer of dawn broke high on the cliffs above them they had broken up the third fight between their dogs and were at the brush heap on the frozen creek where they had turned back the evening before. It was light enough by then to follow the right trail up the creek past their unpleasant surprise of the day before and on to where it climbed the cliff up to the level plateau, like usual, and see how it disappeared there as the long dawn stretched gold along the southern horizon. It was forty-nine below zero, but for once not the slightest wind; not a grain of snow moving. The track had been wiped away during the night.

With nothing but the impressionless ridged snow of the tundra facing them, they boiled tea and then they followed the usual tracker pattern: cast around in a gigantic circle, hoping somewhere, anywhere, to intercept a footprint. One team and two men went west, the others north, one mile, two miles in the heavy cold as the immense livid bulge of the sun emerged on the tundra: January 29, the sun was coming back more and more. Incredibly, two shots very close together. Millen and Riddell raced north, not daring to hope, but hopeful when they heard nothing more.

They found themselves unbelievably lucky. In the very first creek bed Thompson and Lang touched in their circle they had found Johnson's trail. Now they all edged down that together, well spread out; and the sun was clear of the horizon (they could see it from the shallow creek bed) when they discovered the remains of his campfire under the overhang. There were broken rabbit bones sucked for marrow, and the shape of a body on hides dug in against the snow of the cliffs. The mark of the huge pack. Lang scraped away snow, pulled out a charred log.

"He just left," he said very quietly.

"He . . . he heard our shots," Thompson's whisper cracked, his excitement—or was it apprehension, Millen could not be sure—jumping in his face.

"Yeah," Millen turned, looked down the creek. "He's gone there, and he can cut off and up any minute . . . if we're very quiet . . ."

"We should maybe leave the dogs, eh?" Riddell asked.

Millen looked at Lang and nodded. "Right. Come on."

They staked the dogs quickly and moved down the creek. The two policemen went ahead along either bank and the other two followed, widely separated and alert. For a time Millen did not feel the cold; he was concentrating on Johnson, the outline of where he had slept and the incredible size of that pack. just the bedroll alone—he had no eiderdown, it was hide and blankets—must weigh forty pounds, and the clumsy snowshoes—good webbing for this creek snow, but probably bent willow. What possessed him, what drove him this way, endlessly in circles? This was a Bear Creek tributary, no more than eight or ten miles at most from the Rat where his cabin had stood and no matter how good he was this tiny circle of wilderness would eventually give him away, it would have to—if the cold didn't get him first. Or hunger. No one could live in a tent in this cold all winter; and Johnson was without even that.

Millen was aware of the cold then, heavy like clamps screwing in tight, all the time, relentlessly, felt his body moving well but sweating a little too inside his worn caribou clothes, from excitement maybe, or the swing, long swing of his legs and he looked over at Thompson: along the opposite creek bank and heaving himself through a drift, snowshoes tossing the snow aside as his body worked. After all these days he still had that quick, sharp energy of the new arrival, all the backlog of recruit training and young enthusiasm of an entire short lifetime to carry him: if this patrol lasted much longer that could be broken. And then, if he didn't have enough to get past the inevitable sag into the mature conditioning of a northern body and head, this could ruin him, young as he was. Last night had been a near thing: they had to find Johnson soon, or certainly send Thompson back with Eames on the next—he did not want to think into that endless repetition and endless—they should stop for a fire and tea, another ten minutes.

His eye caught: held. The trail of those unmistakable snowshoes turned sharply in front of him, scrabbled up the bank to the low bush of a dry ravine on his right—he wheeled to Thompson but the constable had already noticed the bend of the tracks and was coming towards him quickly across the middle of the creek. Running in his snowshoes, each foot driving down hard and the two men far behind him coming too. And suddenly an explosion, CRACK!

The ice split. One great sheet of thin ice heaving both up and down as Thompson staggered, lost his balance in an immense boil of fast black water bursting up around him and he fell, head and shoulders plunging down and then his snowshoes gesturing desperately for an instant, and everything gone.

"Paul!"

Millen leaped forward but caught himself before he hit the thin crust of snow and the vicious water slanting openly downward there. Thompson had disappeared—in swift water under the ice. Frantically Millen smashed at the thin crust with his rifle butt: Lang and Riddell were there and he screamed at them, and they hammered at the thicker ice before them—how far had Thompson been swept, where, dearest god—and then out of the ice cakes bobbing up by a rock like a prayer was a dark head, Thompson half drowned, gasping, and Millen leaned forward, reckless for himself of any ice or snow crust now and jabbed his rifle between Thompson and the deadly edge of it.

"Here—grab it—here, here!"

And Thompson groped blindly, got his arms up in the staggering tear of water and by a miracle caught a hand in the rifle strap. He clung there and Millen heaved him to his feet. Thompson swayed, coughing desperately chest deep among the ice cakes of the fast water.

Then Lang and Riddell reached them, they were all three hoisting him up onto the solid surface. And into the air; even as they lifted him into the ferocious cold his clothes were turning to ice.

"Quick," Millen gasped, "start fires, I'll keep him moving, quick."

Lang and Riddell turned, ran. Millen tore Thompson's hood back and jerked off the soaked woollen tuque; the young constable was spastic, almost sinking in prostration but Millen kept heaving him up and shouting at him, "On your feet, move, here's my tuque, dry your head, yes, now run, come on! Running on the spot!"

Millen was pummelling Thompson's back, muscling him around as his clothes quickly, silently shaped themselves into a cone of ice over his body.

"Run, on the spot, run!"

While Lang kept feeding the three huge fires they built against the creek bank, Millen and Riddell broke the parkas and pants off Thompson, stripped him down to his woollen underwear. That was almost dry in splotches: the water had not been able to work through all his clothes, but they had to roll that off him too and then they each stripped off their woollen shirts to dry him, vulnerable and naked and leaning almost into the fire, shivering uncontrollably. Finally Millen bundled him into his own underwear. By then they had enough wood together and Lang could run back for his team.

"I just wore this," Millen said cheerfully, getting Thompson's feet into the greyish wool, "about two weeks . . . all my heat's stored up in here."

"More your sweat," Riddell wrinkled his nose, still chafing Thompson's chest and shoulders. "That won't help . . . nothing."

Millen pulled the underwear high. "Huh!" he sniffed at Riddell. "That's Irish energy you smell, undistilled Irish energy!"

"I wish you'd distil it then."

They both chuckled, and Thompson suddenly stuttered: "I . . . sorry I . . . we're so close . . . I didn't listen . . . the water."

"Just don't get frost-bitten or sick," Millen was buttoning the underwear swiftly up his bluish torso.

"I'm very . . . well, thank you," Thompson shivered, and then they all laughed aloud.

In the long twilight an hour later Millen was heating water while Thompson, bundled in masses of clothing, sat inside the heat reflected from the bank and a canvas barrier. His clothes steamed on makeshift racks around the other fire.

"Pretty hard to believe here," Millen said, "but half the people in the world have never even seen ice."

Thompson stared at him incredulously.

"Sure," Millen continued. "I met a guy who went up the Amazon. He couldn't make people there believe it could get so cold the ground would turn stiff!"

Thompson shook his head, laughed a little. "What if this happened and you were alone out here," he said finally.

"If you didn't get pulled under, you could make it," Millen said. "If your matches were dry."

"But your hands, they'd freeze into blocks of ice."

"You'd have to keep sticking them in the water."

"Every few seconds?" Thompson looked at him puzzled. "And build a fire?"

"Well. . ." Millen fished at the handle of the steaming pot with a stick, "one hand, probably both your feet . . ." he shrugged, lifting the pot, "at forty-nine below you're working on a very small percentage anyway."

He poured two mugs of tea. "If you had your dog team close by . . . there's a trapper at Arctic Red River always carried his hunting knife at his belt, he slashed his lead dog open and used the body warmth to keep his hands thawed. He actually only lost three toes when he fell in, but I don't think he went under, like you."

He handed Thompson the hot mug; the young constable sat shuddering, his eyes blackly open to him.

"Look," Millen said softly, "don't get this country wrong. It's really great up here sometimes, even in winter—the northern lights come out and you're moving with the strength of your own body and you know you're alive and in good caribou clothes you can handle anything, let the damn Arctic throw anything at you and you're like a coiled spring you're so strong, you can take on anything, there's nothing—" he stopped suddenly, grinning a bit sheepishly. "Acland in Edmonton last fall figured I'm a bit Arctic crazy already. But I can't stand his headquarters, just shuffling papers, passing on orders . . ."

"Did he want you there?" Thompson asked.

"Oh yeah," Millen drew the boiling tea long and loud between his teeth. "All I'm saying, don't let this patrol ruin it for you. This patrol's totally abnormal, up here too."

"But I really like . . ." Thompson said earnestly, "working with you like this, all of you."

"This patrol, yeah, the work together is good, even the odd dip in the creek to wake us up, it's the reason for it I—well," Millen hesitated, and saw Thompson's intense young eyes studying him above the tucked blanket. "Look, most of the time being a Mountie up here is making sure people know what they're in for living here, tell people to watch the Indians, they've taught us what we know. The first RCMP came north to help out would-be gold rushers who didn't have the knowledge, the equipment to handle the Klondike. Law up here is, leave people alone if they know what they're doing and not bothering others, help where you can, be there in an emergency, and for damn sure don't create it yourself if you can help it. There's lots of space here for everyone, so don't push people, see? Once in a while you break up a drunken fight or something and you cool them down in jail overnight and next morning they start working off their fine breaking trail for your team on a two-week patrol. Like Noel Verville, best man you could want with you on patrol, I had him in for three days plus fine in October. Drunkenness, fighting about a woman, I never asked him what."

"You'll never arrest Lang like that, I bet," Thompson grinned.

"Lang!" Millen laughed. "He can outstare the devil as easy as Martin Luther—women or liquor, he's immovable."

Thompson laughed until he coughed.

"Okay, just don't think Arctic police work is usually like this. It isn't. And man," Millen was pensive abruptly, looking into his tea mug like a memory, "you haven't seen anything till you see a caribou herd on the move. A year ago northwest along the Firth River we saw one, it took three days to pass our camp, forty or sixty thousand I'd say, it was like a grey ocean moving, a forest of antlers and their nice pointed heads and big eyes shining . . . the whole tundra moving. And the click, click double click of their hooves, night and day, for three days. Tundra lice, the Indians call them."

They sat for a long moment in silence; watching steam rise between their cupped hands.

"Think we should call off this patrol?" Millen asked quietly.

Thompson looked at him startled. "The Mounties never . . ." and then he understood. "If we stopped pushing him now, he might give himself up, later?"

"Yeah. He might."

Thompson said, very thoughtfully, "The whole world's watching us."

Millen sat in heavy agreement. "There's some MP in Ottawa asking questions right now. Yeah. It used to be good, being a policeman here," he added after a moment. "You had time to talk to people, learn things, talk them out of hurting themselves, and you. But now there's that goddamn radio connection south and we boxed him in, coming with guns and then blowing up his place. I . . ."

But he did not continue. He could not: because he had not been able to think past that, because he still could not grasp what had started Johnson's implacable, absolute defiance, though he was certain now they had done enough to him after that first encounter to harden him forever somehow, horribly, into whatever rage he already had when he floated into Fort McPherson. He was so angry, there; he could not always have been that. But the sprung trap should have warned him that a few months alone had not changed Johnson. It should have told him, that. Maybe made him worse.

"Why don't you want the plane?" Thompson asked. "It could have got me out to Aklavik in thirty minutes, none of all this—" He gestured at the fires, the steaming clothes.

Millen got up, and started turning the clothes on their racks.

"Sure," he said, "it could." He folded Thompson's caribou parka over; it was clear the younger man had not understood that argument. "If it was here at the right minute, but look, machines . . . Johnson's alone, eh? Not even a dog. He's doing it himself, breaking that trail, sometimes two miles to our one, and living like he can and he's carrying every bit of everything he's got on his own back."

Lang came around the fire with his huge arms full of wood; he dumped it beside Millen.

"Sure," the big Norwegian said. "And why is he doing it?"

"It must be some big reason," Thompson said.

"What I'm saying, it's big enough for him!" Millen leaned forward intensely, "We don't know him, we somehow hit him too hard at the beginning and we boxed him in, Paul, and that's what a cop should never, never—"

Lang stiffened suddenly, then reached for his rifle. Immediately Millen had wheeled, was looking downstream to the bend. Riddell was there, coming up the creek fast, waving.

"He must'a found something," Lang said.

Riddell was panting white as he came up, running on his shoes. "I found him. . . . I found him!"

"Johnson?" Millen asked, "for sure?"

Riddell was already on his knees and scratching a map on the snow between the fires. "The tracks disappeared up there on the tundra like usual so I took a wide circle, about three miles and cut as far south as the Rat River, and then I smelled smoke. There's a steep canyon this way, upstream on that small creek runs into the Rat above the Barrier River, and when I got along it I saw smoke, a tiny wisp. I got right above him, he's under a tarp against the cliff!"

"You're sure it's him?" Millen was already shrugging into his trail clothes.

"Yeah! Hidden right against the cliff. Without the smoke I'd never seen it."

"About half an hour light left," said Lang doubtfully.

"We've got to get a watch on him."

Thompson said anxiously, "You gonna start something before my pants are dry?"

"We'll try to wait till morning," Millen grinned at him. "Come on, Bob, show me where he is."

"How about I come later, eh?" Lang was very concerned.

"We'll just pinpoint him," Millen said, already going. "And Bob will come back for, you about midnight. We can't let him out of our sight again."

"That's for goddamn sure," Lang said, and they all looked at him in surprise. "Well," the trapper said, refusing to be embarrassed, "to get him under my rifle, that'd be worth one real good swear."

Millen and Riddell crunched away, laughing white explosions into the frigid air.

# 16

DAWN NEXT MORNING was an ominous racing of clouds, high and livid with the coming light to a rising wind. The creek canyon was narrow, and high: there was very little space for either cover or strategy.

"We'll watch for you on the cliff," Millen said to Riddell and Lang, "signal as soon as you get in position."

"What if he comes down at you," Riddell said, "before we get up? We can't see him from there, under the tarp, until he comes right out."

"If he comes out, come back fast or shoot, as it develops," Millen said. "Good luck."

"Yeah," Lang nodded his big serious head. "You too." And they were both going.

"See you," Thompson said.

He seemed totally recovered; as he had told them that morning, he was the only one who had had a bath in three weeks so of course he was in better shape than any of them. Now he and Millen worked over their rifles one last time.

"They still tell you that in recruit camp?" Millen asked, "The police are always in the advance? Civilians and special constables, when absolutely necessary, to be used for back-up only?"

Thompson nodded; a bit nervous perhaps but he would do, Millen knew, he'd be fine.

"Well, with you here, for once I can follow the Regina rules."

They moved softly up the canyon towards the cliffs that thrust out of the stunted brush and trees beyond. The wind high above on the plateau was rising: they could hear it whine there, already moving snow uneasily. Millen led along the well-worn track they had made watching that night; to rocks and brush where an open space fanned upwards, suddenly, to the base of the cliffs. They hunched down.

"There," Millen whispered. "The grey tarp, just above that log, by the rocks."

Thompson peered ahead. He had to study the rocks a moment to even recognize a tarp: it was a very good place, for Johnson.

"Why's he staying there," Thompson asked, "so late in the morning?"

"He doesn't know we're anywhere near him . . . maybe he's waiting for the blizzard."

Thompson looked skyward anxiously, "Yeah, it doesn't look so good."

Millen touched his arm. There was a movement against the tarp, a faint shuffle and then suddenly a man's figure lifted itself erect above the log. A rifle in his hand, a huge pack on his back as if he were about to move fast. But he stood there in the open studying the high cliff opposite him.

"If he's heard them . . ." Millen muttered, and cocked his rifle. Thompson was staring at the winter-worn man above him as an apparition; for a month he had been labouring after this man in inhuman cold and darkness and now that he actually saw him, he could not quite believe the simple physical fact of this abrupt appearance. He looked too ordinary and, after a moment, too awesomely tough.

And alert. His head was moving slightly, and then his rifle began to rise slowly. There was a whine like frigid air ripping and Johnson staggered: the cliff above crashed with a rifle explosion. Johnson dived as if hit, vanished behind the log.

Several more bullets whined, thudded into the log as the sounds went hammering over and over each other up the narrow ravine.

Millen was literally jerking with fury. "The stupid idiots . . . the goddamn stupid . . . Riddell!" he roared, "Lang!"

The shooting stopped to his re-echoing voice.

Thompson hunched forward, "Should we charge him now—"

"No! Stay down!"

There was no movement by the tarp and the log.

"They wrecked it . . . ugggh!" Millen could have torn someone apart.

"Wasn't he hit?" Thompson whispered.

Slowly, beside Thompson's innocent sincerity, Millen choked down his rage. "Did he drop, or dive?" he said.

"I . . . I thought he dropped."

"Hard to say," Millen muttered.

"So, what do we . . . ?"

"We wait, especially if he's hit. Let the cold stiffen him a little."

"That's . . ." Thompson hesitated, the word "cruel" in his tone but he stopped it. The momentary physical sight, at last, of the man they had chased as it seemed forever and not once so much as caught a glimpse of, had unnerved him, he knew suddenly. A policeman must always be clear—he thought of those good lectures by grey-haired officers—about what he is doing because he knows the law and the law is untouchable, impartial to all. Excitement, confusion, rashness, that is not worthy of the law, but sometimes swift action . . .

"He's up there, we've seen him," Millen said, hard. "And we're making damn sure, this time."

Behind the log, under the grey tarp that hid the camp from the cliffs above, Johnson's motionless figure lay across the black remains of his tiny fire. He lay sprawled, face down under his huge pack, with his left arm doubled under him and his right stretched out. His right hand still clutched the Savage 30-30.

"Johnson!" Millen's voice bellowed in the canyon all around, "Albert Johnson! This is Spike Millen. You are surrounded!"

The body remained motionless, but the left arm had moved. At the voice. The left arm was moving almost imperceptibly from under the body, it had shifted out from under the pack strap and was moving out, free of the pack, up towards the motionless head still down in the snowy ashes of the fire.

And even more imperceptibly, the right hand with the rifle moved. Forward, slowly and inevitably like a minute-hand moving. The head and body lay as still as the log, but when the rifle reached the left hand it would be in an exact position to shoot anything coming over the log.

Behind the brush below Lang was trying to explain to Millen.

"And then he started bringing up his rifle, and he's such a dead shot we were sure he had seen you and . . ."

Millen interrupted, "He'd heard you—point is, did you hit him?"

"I had him in my sights and—"

"His chest?"

"Yeah," Lang said, totally depressed, "but I . . ." he could only shrug. "I don't know, Spike, I don't."

"There's nothing moving up there," Thompson reported.

"There won't be," Millen glared up at the blowing sky. "We'll just have to wait now, as long as we can."

"Shouldn't Eames be back soon?" Lang asked.

"If four men can't—" Millen broke off. "If you didn't hit him he'll be gone in the storm, that's sure."

Lang nodded heavily; Thompson looked at Millen's black face, then at Lang in sympathy.

They waited until the daylight faded into the grey, coming storm. It had grown steadily colder as the wind gathered itself, and if Johnson was alive up there he must be rigid from the cold. The log and the tarp remained, so innocent in themselves, but so potentially lethal that for a moment Millen could say nothing when Thompson asked, warming his hands and face at the tiny fire they built, "How can you know a man, if he never talks?"

"Well," Millen said after a while, "mostly what he does, I guess."

"He's not even doing anything now."

"Hard to say. I heard him whistle last night."

"Whistle?"

"Just one little tune. Actually sort of tuneless, over and over."

"I thought he never made a sound," Thompson said, strangely.

"He's got a lifetime inside himself; hidden from us."

"But he isn't running away from us either."

"Yeah," Millen said slowly. "He's walked around us, never more than a few miles away. Why doesn't he go, eh Paul, just get as far away as he can?"

Thompson was about to answer, eager to say something he too had been pondering for days, but just then Riddell, across the fire, raised his rifle. Lang appeared behind them from the cliffs. His face was hoared with frost, shivering inside his caribou skins.

"Half an hour, that's all," he said.

"The storm's up there already, eh?" Millen shook himself. "Okay Bob, five minutes for you to get up there."

"If he moves a foot under that tarp," Riddell said, going, "I've got him."

"Okay. Shoot if you can get a shot. Don't miss."

They smothered the fire with snow and got ready again.

"Johnson," Millen shouted up at the log already streaked by driving flakes, "Give yourself up! Come out, give yourself up!"

And they waited, but nothing moved.

"Okay," Millen said finally, "Knut, you stay back and wide right, Paul, the same on the left."

"Do we wait," Thompson said, "for him to shoot first?"

Millen looked at Thompson; he was so young, and innocent.

"No orders, Paul. You use your judgement, whatever happens."

Millen stood up and stepped out into plain view of the log. He glanced to the cliff through the snow swirling up there: Riddell waved to him.

"Johnson!" Millen shouted.

But there was nothing. Millen gestured with his rifle and began to climb through the snow up the slope; Thompson and Lang moved up, slightly behind him, wide, rifles ready.

This is stupid, Millen was thinking, to walk straight up against a rifle that was, as Bill Nerysoo said, just part of him like his arm or his eye. A modern police force should know something better than this frontal business with lead. Like a ridiculous Hollywood western, all guts and no brain. Against a *nana'?ih?* A man, and what was there to do now except walk up, the storm and the darkness an absolute deadline and if you had the moral weight, the personal strength, the man couldn't pull the trigger. He had experienced that; they were lying there sometimes crying behind their doors waiting for you to shove the door open, for the touch of a hand, for a voice that understood, a human being, though he could not believe that of Johnson, probably now nothing but a rigid body lying there, though he could not quite believe that either, one quick shot and Johnson with that deadly rifle, already stiff—he could not believe any of that, or feel it, there was something heavy, black behind that log, and there were just four of them, maybe Johnson—

He could see a hump: the hump of the pack. He stretched up, lurching forward and then he knew as certainly as a heart jolt. Johnson was face down in the snow, the backs of his legs unnaturally bent, and he gestured to Thompson slightly behind him and left, almost wildly, no time to understand the tangle of his emotions now—the poor stupid bugger, they had hounded him—he stopped as in the corner of his eye Thompson came up fast on the left and he barked, suddenly,

"Johnson!"

Over the centre of the log burst that glaring head and the rifle and the shot, all in the same instant.

The canyon exploded with sound as Thompson was hurled backwards. Millen shot fast, he had had his rifle down too low he knew instantly and he fired again, no time to aim as the 30-30 and the ferocious glaring head swung towards him and he dived down as he felt his left arm sting suddenly numb, heard Lang roaring aloud, shooting, and Riddell firing too. Bullets whined against the cliff, the tarp thudded and behind the log, Millen saw as he snapped his head out of the snow and dashed his eyes clear, Johnson jerk high doubled over as if hammered by a bullet and fall far back into the shelter of the cliff.

Lang bellowed in triumph and leaped forward from behind the rock where he had been shooting. And immediately a 30-30 bullet ripped past him and clanged against the far cliff.

"Knut!" Millen yelled, "cover me, I have to get Paul!"

Lang dropped behind the rock again.

"Okay, go! Go!" He was shooting steadily up at the log and the tarp. And Riddell was shooting down.

Millen started to crawl, and immediately collapsed. His left arm . . . the sleeve was ripped and the long red line . . . he hooked his right arm through his rifle strap and dragged himself forward with his right hand and churning knees, ploughing towards that heap down before him, gasping in pain and apprehension, that heap so horribly motionless.

"Paul . . . Paul . . ."

He was beside him and got his bare hand burrowed up inside Thompson's parka, moved it, hesitated, slipped a little there.

He lay then against Thompson, quite still. Around, over him the shots continued, only Lee-Enfields, no 30-30; he was aware of that. The wind howled fiercely lower between the funnelling cliffs. After a long moment of rifles barking Millen roused himself and moved to Thompson's feet. His left arm hung useless and he worked at the long laces of Thompson's moccasins with his bare right hand, loosened both of them, and tied the separate laces together with his hand and teeth.

Rooting his face down into the hard snow, his hand too as if he would bury himself, hammer himself past pain into some frozen world beyond feeling. Then he hooked his right arm through the tied laces and began to drag Thompson backwards through the snow. Away from the shooting.

Riddell met him when he got to their dead campfire. The storm drove down fiercely at them, and the signalman hunched over him and bandaged his bloody arm quickly in the lee of his body.

"Just stop the bleeding . . . for now . . ." Riddell muttered, trying to make the stiffening tape stick. Millen flexed his fingers, gasped with pain, but they all worked.

"Always under the left arm," Riddell said, "King, you . . ."

He hesitated. Millen looked at Thompson's body; the head had dropped aside, he could not see the face.

"That's because you're sideways to him," Riddell could not stop talking, "about to shoot and he always goes for the—"

Lang emerged out of the whistling snow and Riddell stopped. The big trapper looked at Thompson's body stretched out, and feet tied together; there was no need to ask anything.

"I can't see a thing by his cliff," Lang said slowly. "We better get to base camp fast."

Millen pushed Riddell's busy fingers aside and stood up. He pulled the torn sleeve of his parka down, picked his rifle out of the snow with his right hand. He grunted, but he got his left hand into his mitten; it would be usable if he could stand the pain.

"Spike," Lang said, "you can't, the—"

Millen was looking from him to Riddell, still on his knees and staring up, with a terrible ferocity. He did not raise his voice in the shrieking wind.

"You both stay here. I don't want to kill you by mistake."

He cocked the rifle awkwardly with one hand, turned up the slope. He walked without care, stumbling, almost falling several times and approaching the log head-on through the white storm; and he stepped over it and kicked the tarp up; it caught in the wind and snapped aside. Nothing. No pack, nothing. He stepped through to the cliff face behind it, a corner, how . . . and then he put his face closer to the cliff.

There were notches hacked up the frozen rock; moccasin prints, slips of snow on them.

He looked up; the cliff with its footholds disappeared into the dark streaking storm. He struggled into his rifle strap, put his hands there and tried to lift himself: again, and again, but he could not hold his weight. His left arm would not take any pressure.

He collapsed. Down in a huddle against the frozen rocks. But his face came up and it was running with tears and he was bellowing upward against the cliff into the blizzard,

"You devil! Johnson! Johnso-o-nnn!"

*Part Four*

# The Second Manhunt: Mountains and Sky

# 1

THE BLIZZARD THAT BROKE over them was the worst they had faced all that terrible month, but an unstoppable Knut Lang tramped out a trail across tundra plateau and through ravines to base camp on the Barrier River and brought Riddell and the exhausted dogs in with Millen riding one sled and Thompson's body lashed down on the other. By then it was nearly noon of Sunday, January 31, and Eames had returned from Aklavik. With fifteen men and nine dog teams digging down to outlast the blizzard, it was like a small Arctic town now, double-walled tents and fires and howling dogs. Eames' command tent was carefully piled over with snow and brush, almost comfortable despite the cold and knifing wind outside. It was there he washed the long bullet gash on Millen's arm and sewed it together.

"You did fine," he said to the gaunt Riddell holding a basin of bloody water and needles. "No infection, you kept it clean."

"Too damn cold for germs I guess," Riddell said without humour.

Millen was examining his slit caribou sleeve closely; he had no expression, not even exhaustion, on his unshaven, cold-blotched face.

"Okay," Eames said to Riddell, winding a bandage around Millen's muscular arm, "you go get some sleep, you've earned it."

"No," Riddell said, "I have to help Frank, on the radio."

"You sure you can do it?"

"Another hour won't matter, I'll sleep then."

"Okay," Eames said. "Hersey knows what Aklavik's supposed to send Acland in Edmonton about this; make sure that gets through first.

Then, they keep radioing all across the Mackenzie and northern Yukon, every morning, noon, evening, three messages. One: if anyone meets Erickson, he's got to report in right away; two: every trapper, everywhere, report any strange track, any distant figure, smoke, anything; three: we want volunteers, everyone who possibly can, to join us on the Barrier River to hunt Johnson. Got that?"

"First Acland, then the north: Erickson, any unusual sign, volunteers."

"Right. We're okay here now." Eames was snipping off the bandage. "Go get those messages through."

Riddell put down the basin, tugged his hood over his head and bent out into the howling snow. Eames wiped his hands.

"Thank god, Hersey's got that radio working well now."

Millen said nothing. Eames began repacking his medicine kit, glancing up occasionally, but Millen kept turning the sleeve of his slashed parka over and over in his right hand; silently.

"I don't know what Acland is doing," Eames said loudly, "but they can't seem to find anything of Johnson's family. Nothing, he says, absolutely nothing has come up, they've had messages out for weeks. They've followed three leads, one in BC about a Johnson in Prince George, but it was obviously the wrong man. I can't understand why they can't trace something that would help us."

Millen said, abruptly, "There's no point bringing all those trappers here."

Eames paused. "What?" he asked.

"Johnson isn't here anymore."

Eames stared at him. "Nobody," he said finally, "nobody could cross the Richardson Mountains in this blizzard."

"Johnson will."

"What for?"

"Get across the Yukon to Alaska."

Eames hesitated, then closed the medicine kit. He took Millen's parka out of his hand and helped him into it.

"That bandage should hold you," he said, working a big pin through the slashed underwear sleeve, "till we get you to Doc Urquhart."

"Alex," Millen said without any expression in his voice or face, "I'm in this to the finish."

"If you get infected you'll—"

"I won't get infected,"

There was an immovable set on Millen's face that had nothing to do with either logic or human feelings; or a superior's orders. It was simply as implacable as the storm roaring outside.

# 2

IN THE MAGNIFICENTLY PANELLED OFFICE of the Minister of Justice in Ottawa, Royal Canadian Mounted Police Commissioner Sir James MacBrien faced the bald-headed Minister. A dapper man, MacBrien was the most capable leader the police had had since James Macleod in 1875. He was both a brilliant administrator and had great political influence, but now he sat in full dress uniform and listened. Silently.

". . . and that," the Minister waved a single sheet of paper across his massive clean desk, "on the front page of every newspaper and on every radio newscast every hour in the whole country?"

"The radio and the papers, sir," MacBrien said quietly, "are always full of killings, suicides, shoot-outs of all kinds, the—"

"But not where the police are doing them. For five weeks, and getting nowhere, and now an officer killed, from Nova Scotia and young, really, this," he stooped, pulled open a drawer and waved newspapers out of it, "look here, 'Mad Trapper Shoots Young Mountie'; 'Johnson is crazy like a fox'; 'The vengeance of the law must now be' . . . I mean, in the worst Depression this country has ever had, we don't really need this, do we, Commissioner?"

MacBrien opened his mouth to explain the problems his men were facing, but the Minister would brook no interruption.

"How much money has this Johnson business cost so far?"

"Between seven and nine thousand dollars," MacBrien said expressionlessly.

"There are entire families on relief all over Canada living on three dollars a week!"

The single sheet of paper waved MacBrien's protest aside.

"I know, I know," the Minister continued. "But I want answers to things I don't know. Mr. Bennett is asking me questions, Mackenzie King in Opposition is asking me questions, I can't cross the hall without reporters asking me questions—I want answers from you that will shut them up."

"A plane," MacBrien said, "costs over a hundred dollars a day."

The Minister of Justice stooped his large bald head forward across his desk like an eagle bending. MacBrien met his unblinking eye unblinkingly.

"The faster you get him," the Minister said, "the less it costs."

MacBrien stood up immediately, with a slight bow. "Sir," he said.

"And by the way," the Minister said easily, looking sideways through the stone arch of the window, "if things really are so tough for your men, why not gain some sympathy for the police? We could all do with some press sympathy this winter."

MacBrien hesitated, apprehensive. "I . . . don't think I understand you."

"All those reporters are doing now is speculating in their nice warm offices, writing crap and speculating. Well, get them out there where they'll freeze their balls off, right on the hunt."

MacBrien stood rigid, his mouth fallen open.

# 3

SO ON WEDNESDAY, FEBRUARY 3, Captain "Wop" May in his usual black tam and outer cloth parka belted tightly over his fur inner one led a gaggle of reporters at a very fast walk across the snow-covered runway of the Edmonton Municipal Airport. Gary Snardon, carrying a bedroll and bag, trotted beside him towards the Bellanca airplane.

"We'll try and go up the usual route I fly mail," May explained to the reporters, "Fort McMurray, Simpson, Norman Wells, Arctic Red River, the Mackenzie to Aklavik."

"How long will it take—"

"How many miles—"

May knew their questions by heart; he had been asked exactly the same ones time and again when he flew the mail north, or returned, but there had never been reporters from Chicago and New York and even Los Angeles to feverishly scribble down his answers, and he laughed at the photographers without breaking stride.

"A bit over one thousand five hundred miles, and I could make it in two days but there's a bad storm moving across now," he shrugged. "You learn how to fly up here, nobody ever said it's not dangerous."

"Where do you land, if a storm forces you down?"

"You hope near a settlement, but you land where you have to. There's lots of level snow, no worry there!"

"Are you taking bombs?" the most persistent reporter asked.

"I have contracted to carry men and supplies for the RCMP."

"Not even rifles?"

May had crunched to the airplane. It stood on its wide skis, idling easily in the cold sunlight. He gestured as the chief mechanic clambered out of the cabin door onto the wing strut. "You see that? Sheer comfort, a cabin Bellanca. When Vic Horner and I flew that diphtheria serum to Fort Vermilion in '29 we damn near froze to death sitting in open cockpits—the comforts of your own living room, this three-hundred horsepower Bellanca."

"You bet!" the mechanic said. "She'll take you anywhere, Wop."

May clamped him on the shoulder. "Thanks, Jack. If she stops on me, I'll walk back and give you holy hell." They laughed together, new men of the air together against the ordinary blokes who could do nothing but walk the earth as they always had.

"Are you carrying dynamite and rifles?" the reporter insisted.

May looked at him coldly. Snardon was already climbing onto the strut.

"I am carrying supplies for the Mounted Police," May repeated as for a child.

"Mr. May, you've been quoted as saying 'You win a war any way you have to.' Are you going up there to fight a war with the Mad Trapper?"

"Like you fought a war with the Red Baron," piped another voice from the shivering crowd. It was twenty-one below in Edmonton that morning.

For a moment May glared; but he changed his mind quickly. "You want to know what I say?"

"Yes." The insistent reporter was obviously cold.

There was a pause; Snardon hesitated in the plane's doorway, looking down on the crowd, listening hard now too.

"I say," May said slowly, "you can go ask Major-General Sir James MacBrien, Commissioner of the Royal Canadian Mounted Police, in Ottawa. He hired me."

He wheeled, jumped on the wing strut; the reporters surged forward.

"Why is Snardon going along?" someone shouted.

May laughed; they were good for him, he knew, and they were also goddamn hyenas. He yelled suddenly, "Read the *Bulletin*. He's gonna tell you . . . how we bring in the Mad Trapper!"

He waved, stepped in and pulled the door shut. In a minute the plane shuddered, slid onto the runway. The reporters ran out of its whirling snow, the photographers knelt, cameras clicking, and not one blue-fingered neophyte moved until the graceful plane had lifted up into the grey sky and curved away northeast. They were seeing history made; they knew.

"Why didn't you mention the tear gas bombs," Snardon asked when they had levelled out, the Bellanca. hammering steadily.

May was busy with gauges. "Huh!" he grunted after a while. "I didn't tell them about my rifle either. Why should I?"

"You gonna . . . shoot Johnson yourself?"

"Look, Gary," May glanced at the reporter swiftly, and his face and eyes were hard, calculating. Shoulder against shoulder, Snardon realized with astonishment he had never seen the pilot like this—what was it—

"This isn't the King Eddy bar. This is Arctic winter flying, that's a blizzard over there and maybe we can get around it, maybe we can't. I fly equipped to do anything I have to to come out alive. Got that?"

Snardon could only look at him. The plane rattled, slipped sideways uneasily, and suddenly Snardon wondered with a jolt of understanding very close to panic how he had ever imagined May flying where he did, a real Air Ace, when all he knew of him was a Sunday swing around over Edmonton and Strathcona and under the High Level Bridge (if the paying passenger had the nerve) and occasionally a slightly sloshed talker telling slightly more improbable stories than anyone else in the bar. For this, this bottomless shifting, this hanging on nothing really in the rolling air, space, this was where this man lived, where he went as regularly as others stepped out of their front doors, good god in heav—

"And if I don't make it," May muttered, "you sure as hell won't either."

Snardon was suddenly absolutely certain of that.

# 4

THE RICHARDSON MOUNTAINS form the boundary between the Northwest Territories and the Yukon. They are the northernmost extension of the Rockies, the final rise of the mountain backbone of North America before it disappears under the Beaufort Sea of the Arctic Ocean. Mosses, lichens, flowers like the pin pricks of a rainbow grow on the barren rocks of their unglaciated slopes during late June and July and early August, but at other times they are battered by storms and staggering cold.

The blizzard that drove southeast from beyond Barrow, Alaska, and across the Yukon and the Mackenzie valley and down through the centre of the continent to finally lose itself on the plains of Oklahoma and Texas, this blizzard roared through the Richardson Mountains for six days. It was during these days that Albert Johnson climbed into the divide at the head of the Barrier River.

He walked as he always had, head lowered against the wind, changing his rifle from one hand to the other, his enormous pack on his back and lifting and laying down his heavy snowshoes steadily, relentlessly, as if he would never stop. When the blizzard staggered, momentarily eddied into daylight and, as it seemed, caught its breath, he would sometimes glance up to see the peaks about him: the enormous vista of groaning, moving snow, the ravines and the ice-blasted pyramids that howled dolefully as the blizzard shook itself and howled, howled. But he did not stop; he forced himself steadily ahead, upwards. If he ever stopped moving in that inhuman lethal world, he would never move again.

# 5

THE BELLANCA hammered steadily northwest at one hundred twenty miles an hour. On the first day the blizzard pushed them down at Fort Smith on the border of the Northwest Territories; the next day they made five hundred miles north and west to Fort Simpson. The storm was worse on Friday but they got aloft when ten men pushing got them started on the Mackenzie/Liard River ice, and at four thousand feet they were above the snow but the wind was hurricane force and the temperature outside sixty-seven below. The Mackenzie, outlined by a narrow fringe of trees, wound endlessly through the whiteness below them as the Bellanca slipped sideways, rose and fell.

May kept peering at the heavy banks of cloud to the left. "It seems to be, moving over a bit, maybe we can get past Norman Wells all the way to Aklavik . . . maybe . . . maybe today."

Snardon said nothing. Finally, after three days he was devastated by airsickness.

"One good thing," May said cheerfully, "when you're so sick you don't notice your feet freeze."

The reporter did not think that funny. "I can feel them . . . freeze," he groaned.

"Then rub them. I'm leaving you at The Wells."

Snardon forced himself to bend forward, struggle with his boot-laces. The movement, the bending heaved his stomach in a dreadful roll and for a moment he had to lean back, head lolling and face grey, twitching in misery.

"No . . . no you're not," he managed after a time. "You are not Number Six, Wop."

"What?" May's head jerked around at him.

"You're an Ace . . . sure, and that's gre . . . great, but you got into the War too late, you're not . . . in the top thirty."

May could only stare at him.

"Bishop had seventy-two kills," Snardon said with his head back, eyes closed. "You had fourteen."

May's head turned slowly back to his gauges. All was well there, the engine thundered on, the plane sank and rose again.

Loading supplies into May's Bellanca, Aklavik, February 1932

"Thirteen," May said quietly. "What kind of a reporter are you? You think you get facts in bars?"

Snardon pried one boot off with the other, and bent to give his foot a hard rub. But then the plane lurched and he had to reach for the can under his seat, fast.

# 6

EVEN DURING THE BLIZZARD Eames had attempted short patrols in the ravines, but it was not until the storm finally blew out on Friday that they could really work up the unnamed creek above Johnson's cliff camp where Thompson had been killed. He sent out three five-man, two-team patrols on Friday and Saturday, but they found not so much as a single Johnson track. And though more men and dogs began arriving every day—Eames himself had no time to leave base camp now—none of them had seen anything coming in either.

So when they heard the strange drone at noon on Sunday, February 7, everyone left in camp rushed into the open and shaded their eyes against the low sun, staring about. Some of the staked dogs barked in a frenzy, others cowered in terror, for there it was, suddenly, a dot of something out of place and foreign in that silent, bright Arctic sky, growing larger in the northeast to an increasing noise.

"To your stations," Eames shouted. "Light the fires."

The men scattered across the wide snow of the creek bed towards the brushpiles they had prepared. Millen came out of his tent then and stood motionless, watching the Bellanca roar a circle over the sprawling camp while the dogs howled, terrified. His parka sleeve was neatly double-sewn and he kept flexing, working that arm.

The plane circled west, wide, and came in towards the two fires blazing at the far end of the runway. They had tramped it down with snowshoes, fifteen men side by side up and down the creek for half a day and now the plane came smoothly between the fires and touched down as light as ash settling, only its tremendous roar against the river cliffs and the swirl of snow that hid it momentarily like a devilwind touching down destroyed the illusion. Knut Lang waved it forward with his long arms, and it slid in close towards Eames and his cluster of men striding forward. Its sound sputtered down and the propeller gasped to a halt; it stopped sliding.

The door opened. May stepped out on the strut and dropped to the snow.

"Captain May?" Eames said, coming forward.

"Inspector Eames?" said May, smiling broadly and sticking out his hand. They shook. "Fine landing strip, sir, smoother than Aklavik's!"

"You came from Aklavik?" Eames asked.

Snardon was climbing out behind the pilot; his legs were a little wobbly but his face excited looking about the enormous camp, the dark northern men moving about so easily in the cold, the quick sense of action here that not a single reporter had seen before him.

May was digging documents out from under his parka. "Yes sir," he smiled at Eames, "finally got there yesterday, for night, and had a good forty-minute flight out."

"Forty minutes . . ." Eames sighed, not wanting to think of it.

May said, "Here's the messages from Edmonton headquarters, here's the list of supplies on board—"

He stopped, his hand up awkwardly with the papers. Eames was staring behind him.

"Who's that?"

"Inspector Eames," May said with all proper military formality, "I'd like you to meet Gary Snardon of the *Edmonton Bulletin.*"

Snardon stepped forward, smiling, his hand out. "A real pleasure, Inspec—"

Snardon caught on then; Eames was rigid with rage.

"What the—" Eames began, stopped, and then could not control himself, "What the goddamn hell do you think is going on here!"

"A rodeo," Millen said. He had come up silently behind them and stood there studying May.

"What?" May wheeled to Millen.

"We're hunting a dangerous killer, May," Eames barked.

"I know," May was as cold, as official. "And I have here the authorization from your Commissioner, in Ottawa—"

Eames snatched the letter from him, glanced at it and his face suffused red once more. He was cursing under his breath.

"... waste that weight of supplies to ..." he glared at the pilot. "I don't care if you have a letter from God Almighty, just you keep that ..." he gestured but did not voice what he was thinking, "just keep that out of my way! All right," Eames wheeled to the clustered men, "let's get this plane unloaded!"

The silent men moved forward; Snardon had to scramble to get out of their way.

Millen said, "You ever flown over the Richardson Mountains?"

May looked up, and suddenly he grinned. "Hey," he said, "you Spike Millen?"

"Yes."

May's grin broadened into a quick smile. "The world's been hearing about you, Corporal, my pleasure!" He shook hands vigorously. "And I fly anywhere there's air."

"Let's fly then," Millen said without smiling.

# 7

THE RICHARDSON MOUNTAINS had been impossible during the storm, even for Johnson. There was no way for him to judge how close he might be to the top of any pass, not that a pass itself could really matter in this scream of wind and buckshot snow, and in his steady tramp the drifts abruptly slid out from under him and he fell down a snowface, sliding, half catching himself on nothing but the sweep of his snowshoes in the avalanche and on nothing and then finally riding downward head up or down, without trying, until he slowed and stopped and found himself caught by a ledge blown clear, his snowshoes snagged on the small brush of a peregrine falcon's nest that perched there above an abyss whose bottom it was impossible to see. And in the folds of icy wind-cleared rocks, a hole; a cave perhaps. He could not resist that, bruised and exhausted beyond all possible exhaustion. He unhooked his snowshoes and squirmed his way down.

It was a cave; almost deep enough and its crevices driven tight with snow. The wind blasting outside made its opening upward act like a chimney and he found he could cook flour with sugar and heat water over a tiny fire of falcon-coated sticks. The smell stung faintly like chickens in his nose as he hunched over it but there was a small warmth there at least. So he could take off his clothes, sweat-soaked and deadly as soon as he stopped moving and he laid them out flat to freeze and pulled his bedroll in tight while the dying fire reflected a hint of light from the ice-coated rocks and snow glistening around him.

When he awoke there was sunlight at the tiny hole in the snow, which was all that was left of the entrance. The light shone crystal bright through the snow, and beyond it the wind whispered easily, almost like a friend. He could barely break out of his bedroll, its hides frozen so stiff, and he did not look at his feet; his hands, curled between his thighs as he slept, could still move and he got his matches from his pack and again began to burn a paper bag he had left and then canvas and a small fire grew of that and worn hide he might have eaten. The only wood he had now was the sawed off stock of the .22: he split that with his skinning knife against the rocks into three pieces, four, and the smouldering canvas got the hardwood edges burning at last though the smoke gathered dangerously. His hands were almost impossible by then, but that saved them and he warmed himself enough to break the ice out of his clothes and beat them soft with his clubbed hands, layer by layer so he could put them on almost dry again and the cave—hole really, the snow driven over it like a bear's hibernation den—perceptibly warmer now. He thawed the last small bit of rabbit in his pack, gnawed it carefully, the fire too low to do more than melt snow so he drank icy water and let mouthful after mouthful of sugar melt in his mouth with that. He swallowed two pills, slowly but without ceremony. Then he waited the wood out; held the coals in his hands to warm them one last time, and broke through the snow drift above the cave, dragging his pack and his rifle up behind him.

His snowshoes stuck like a signal out of the snow on the ledge. That and the rock ledge beside him were the only bits of dark in the entire world. Peak upon great slanted peak glazed white in the bright blue sky; he might have fallen a few more hundred feet straight down, but he did not look there. He stuck the shoes through his pack straps and trudged up along the line of falcon's rock ledge. When he met the snow, he laced on the shoes and continued walking. Sometimes he stumbled; his feet wrenched aside a little but he did not pause. It was clear he did not dare look at his feet until he found some solid warmth.

It was near noon when the long incline of snow suddenly levelled and tilted down before him. He looked up: the mountains eased away in front of him—he had topped the pass.

He leaned against the rocks a moment. A shift of air, almost warm in the dreadful cold, seemed to breathe upward here from the west. And with it . . . he half turned and listened behind him. A sound, but after a moment he put his head down and started walking again.

He was going down now, the mountains on the Yukon side of the pass dropping away in long slanting slopes to a wide plateau. The snow was softer here, not driven hard. He was sinking deeper, leaving a wide obvious trail. He kept on moving however, steadily west, his snowshoes plucking up tufts of soft snow at each step. There was the cut of a river below him on the plateau, and along the river there would be brush, perhaps even a tiny old tree.

# 8

THE BELLANCA with May at the controls and Millen seated beside him, sketchy maps spread out over his knees, was flying straight towards the white peaks of the Richardson Mountains. As far as could be seen, left and right, the pyramid ranges stretched before them in the dazzling light.

May kept glancing up and then quickly back to his gauges again. "I can't do it," he said after a few minutes. "They're too high, we'll have to go between them somewheres."

"There's a pass," Millen said, reading maps, "left, only five thousand feet."

May glanced down at his finger, then banked sharply left. Despite the unnerving sideways slips of the plane in the mountain air currents, the policeman rode his belted seat as if it were a living-room rocker. And the first line of peaks was beside them now, desolate and awesome. May shook his head, looking down.

"God himself couldn't walk over that," he said.

"There." Millen pointed sharp right. A pass perhaps, the suggestion of river canyons cutting into ledges and higher slopes, pyramids, below them. May banked right, uneasily.

"Well," he said and laughed a bit as he opened the motor another notch. "If it's too high . . . we'll just have to back up."

Millen was scraping ice off the side window, trying to stare beyond his own hoaring breath at the blank snow rising gradually to meet them. He did not so much as glance at the peaks edging in closer with each hammering revolution of the Bellanca's straining engine.

The snow down the Yukon slope of the Richardsons was heavier, deeper in the warmer air that softened it. Johnson was ploughing a trail, but he thudded on around outcrops and down slopes, sucking rabbit bones while his snowshoes maintained their implacable, distance-eating rhythm.

But suddenly he stopped. He knocked back his parka hood, shifted his wool cap aside and listened. There was an undeniable drone in the mountains behind him and he looked frantically about, everywhere. But there was nothing; only the rocks and the silent, motionless slopes . . . and his ploughed track pointing at him like an arrow in the snow.

And the terrible sound. Growing louder, droning nearer sourcelessly and invisibly like some enormous roaring beast snoring him out. He could not tell what it was or from where it was coming but at any instant now it would burst upon him like an explosion on the open snow slope and he wheeled and began to run. On his snowshoes, lunging ahead desperately, a scrabbling black dot on the blank betrayal of the enormous slope. He staggered to a stop, but the drone bouncing off the peaks seemed almost above him now, the sky innocent and deadly, only the sound and he sprinted panic-stricken along rocks in his clumsy snowshoes. Their webbing shredded under him as the sound hammered up, he staggered, tripped, sprawled on his face with arms outspread, his now useless rifle still clutched in his right fist.

May was sweating it out as the Bellanca lurched, threaded upwards in the narrow pass. It was too high, the slope rising too fast and the peaks tightening, the currents could throw them sideways into—and suddenly an immense flank rock loomed where a passage should be, had to be, had to.

"Millen . . . Millen," May muttered, eyes flicking from gauge to windshield and back, "I don't think . . . I can't . . ."

Millen was concentrating ahead as if his stare would force a passage, if they could not lift they would be splattered, at best draped like hung wires.

"Right!" Millen said sharply, "there, right!"

A narrow pass opened and the straining plane banked, slid sideways into it. They roared on aslant with the rock flank barely beyond the tip of their wing.

"Huhh. . ." May groaned in relief; there was open sky and the space of falling slopes before them. "Another one like—"

"Down!" Millen exploded. "Get down, down!"

"What?" May gasped.

Millen was straining his forehead against the window.

"There's tracks, down, I can see . . . tracks!"

"Holy . . . !" and May nudged the plane down. He could see a slur in the snow, yes, ploughed deep and for a moment he was totally on instinct as he had been so often fighting over France years before or feeling his way through blizzards and the frozen waste of Arctic: the Bellanca was an extension of himself, he was nothing but eye and arms outstretched and he was walking himself through air and he knew his skis were two, or perhaps five feet off the snow and at this speed—

"Slow down!" Millen roared, "I can't see, slower!"

"If I slow, I'll stall!"

"Then stall!"

But at that instant May saw looming black rocks. Dead ahead and he hurled the plane up in reflex, the last ounce of power as the Bellanca vibrated, shuddered, but lifted like his body heaving itself up, and the bare rocks and snow lurched, fell away below them.

Johnson lay flat under his grey pack among the rocks. He was completely open to the sky and as the sound descended on him like an avalanche he clutched the back of his head with his hands, his rifle forgotten. He cowered, the roar lifted over him as if the very earth were blowing apart, its vibrations blasting him with ice wind, and then it faded, quickly down the valley west.

Johnson's head moved at last. His face was gashed from falling among the rocks, and only then did he see the plane. A small dot retreating into the white distance of sky.

Slowly he pushed himself to his feet. One snowshoe was shredded off his feet, the other held only a ripping of lace. He stopped to pick up his rifle when the distant sound of the plane changed.

He stared into the brightness towards it. It was turning; it would come back. Seeing everything from the sky.

And then, abruptly as always, Johnson's body leaped out of fear, exhaustion, into fury. For an instant it seemed his worn leather clothes would burst with it, he was waving his rifle and kicking his snowshoes loose and screaming, his entire controlled world so destroyed by the uncontrollable suddenly, and he grabbed the shoes and ran between the open jagged rocks where he had lain.

The thunder of the plane bored at him, its blank mechanical face coming there and his rage splintered back into fear: he threw himself behind rocks.

The plane hammered over him. Oblivious, back into the pass.

Johnson lay still, very much as he had lain behind the log. And for a long time not even his arms moved, slowly.

# 9

A CLUSTER OF MEN waited beside the supply dump as the Bellanca came in smoothly on the river ice. Snardon was there behind the dark-coated posse, his notebook out and already scribbling.

"He did cross the mountains," Millen said jumping off the strut as Eames came up to him. He held the sheaf of maps in his hand.

Eames could not believe it. "You . . . you saw his tracks?" he asked at last. Riddell, Hersey, Lang were there, and May ducking under the wing past Snardon.

"It's tough tracking at eighty miles an hour," May laughed, "but the tracks are there, in soft snow. Through the pass and on the other side."

Eames was looking at Millen. Despite this incredible discovery, there was no satisfaction or relief in his face. No emotion whatever. There had not been since Thompson was shot; simply this blank inwardness.

"We have to get between him and Alaska," Millen said.

"Yes," Eames said slowly, and Millen handed him the maps, already open to the right sheet. The men pushed forward, looking at the map but Eames held it, not looking at it, just thinking.

"It'll take at least two days to get over by dog team," Lang said. "That's a hell of a tough country."

"But we'll have to move camp into the Yukon?" Hersey asked.

"Yes," Eames said, "yes we have to move there—"

"Not even Johnson," Lang said, taking the maps and pointing at distances, "can get across all that Yukon in one day."

"May," Eames said suddenly, "you fly three trackers across right now and the rest of us will break camp and—"

"I'm sorry, sir," May said, uncomfortably. "I can't, I—"

"What?"

"Gas. With those ten-gallon cans I can just make Aklavik."

Eames swore, glaring at the pilot.

"Tomorrow with full tanks, I'll get you there in minutes, but right now . . ."

"No . . ." Eames was recovering himself. "Knut's right, he can't get across the Yukon in one day." He pointed at the map the signallers had unrolled between them. "There, La Pierre House, on the Bell River, there. First thing tomorrow stockpile a full load of gas there, then come back here and get the trackers over."

"Sure," May said quickly, "sure."

"Meanwhile, the dog teams can start at 4 AM, and Lazarus can get us through over the Stony Creek trail in two long days."

Lang was nodding his big head. "Yeah, use La Pierre House for a base. Cut him off."

"We should radio all the trappers," Hersey said, "Johnson's in the Yukon."

"Yes," Eames wheeled. "Let's get gas into this plane."

"You can save money," Millen said. "Send half these men home."

Eames hesitated, looked around at him. But Millen had already turned away. He passed Snardon who lifted his hand to ask him something, but when he saw the policeman's face he thought better of it. May was coming past, heading for the stack of supplies.

"Wop," Snardon said, very low. "Wop!"

May looked at him curiously, as if he had forgotten his existence.

"I can't walk across those mountains!"

May grinned; suddenly glad he had brought him along, this pencil pusher.

"Hey, Gary, we're in the Arctic. You don't walk behind dog teams here, you run!"

Snardon stared at him in consternation, and then had to jump aside quickly as a gasoline barrel came rolling, crunching over the snow towards the plane.

# 10

THAT NIGHT the air over the Mackenzie Valley began to warm, and it started to snow. It snowed all day Monday, February 8, and May, pacing, could not budge from Aklavik because he could not see twenty feet beyond his propeller; even if he took off and got above the snow clouds, he had no idea where he could come down, or whether he would be able to find his way back. On Tuesday, however, the snow stopped near noon to a low overcast. Six men dug out the plane and twenty tramped down a runway and he got off the river with a full load and headed for La Pierre House. But there were no passes through the Richardson Mountains that far north and May flew almost two hours, looking, before he could decide on how to get between the six-thousand-foot peaks to the Yukon. He had flown twice the hundred-mile trip by then, and when he crossed back to the Barrier River camp he discovered that flank of the mountains further south was blanketed with wet, low clouds. He made Aklavik, still clear thank god in the five-o'clock darkness, and McDowell had the runway fires burning higher than the houses on the river bank.

So it was Wednesday before he could pick up Millen, Lang and Hersey from the Barrier River camp, and it was well past noon when they landed where the Bell River looped around La Pierre House. Landed in a gently lowering fog.

Two stocky white men left a group of Dene clumped around the gasoline barrels at the river bank and came to meet Millen climbing out.

"Corporal Millen?" one of them asked. "I'm Frank Jackson."

Millen shook the trader's proffered hand. "Hello. Good of you to level off a strip, and let us use your place."

"That's fine, fine, we're glad to be of help, but we're being a bit overrun."

"What's the matter?"

"The Indian people," the trader gestured up the bank, "they're bringing their families in. They say no human being has ever crossed the Richardsons in a blizzard."

Millen shook his head, quickly. "No spirit or *nana'?ih* leaves a trail like that."

The man with Jackson had been listening intently, and he edged forward now. "Corporal," he said, "I'm Karl Erickson and I—"

"Erickson! Why didn't you contact us?"

"I just heard all this, two days ago. Did Bert really . . . kill a Mountie?"

"Yes."

The trapper could only shake his head, in despair. "I waited for him last fall, as long as I—" He shook his head again. "Look, when I was coming in I crossed some strange snowshoe tracks and—"

"What'd they look like?" Millen interrupted.

Hersey and Lang crowded around as Erickson sketched in the snow. "They're really long," he said, "about five feet, and heavy . . . webbing sort of like this."

"Johnson," Lang said, "sure as hell."

"Yeah," Hersey pointed, "that cross piece there."

"Where are they?" Millen asked.

"Fifteen miles southwest."

Lang swore. "He's past us already!"

"Snow doesn't stop him," Hersey said.

"May!" Millen turned and called, "May!"

May had been examining the wings of the Bellanca ever since they landed. He looked up, not moving. Millen walked towards him quickly.

"Take us up," he said. "They've spotted Johnson's trail just fifteen miles out."

But May shook his head grimly. "It's this fog," he said, running his mittened hand along the wing's edge, "you see that, it's icing up, bad."

The trader Jackson offered into the silence as Millen stared at May, "After it snows in the Yukon, it's always warm here."

"Sure," Lang ran his huge bare hand inside his collar, pretending to loosen it, "Capri of the Arctic, right here."

"Capri bullshit!" May barked. "If my wings ice up I—"

"One circle southwest!" Millen exploded angrily.

"And what do I do with you then? I can't land here again today, I'll be lucky if I can get up out of this soup and not come down," and he drove his right fist down hard into his left.

Millen was livid, so furious he seemed about to lunge forward and assault May right there. Lang wouldn't have stopped him, but Hersey stepped forward quickly, placatingly. "It's okay, Spike, one night it's okay. We know where he is, tomorrow Alex with Lazarus and the dogs will be here—"

"And first thing tomorrow," May said, voice unusually small, "hell or high water I'll be here, take you up and we'll find him."

"It often lifts," Jackson said, "with the morning sun."

"Five more minutes flying tomorrow," May said, already going. "He can't hide anywhere out here. Okay, okay?"

Slowly Millen was gaining control of himself. He nodded, and walked away towards the dark gathering of Gwich'in Dene still silent on the bank above them, watching.

# 11

Thursday, February 11 dawned misty with fog. Long before brief daylight Millen had the Dene hauling in brush with their dog teams, and they lit the fires at ten o'clock. Then he sat like a stone in the log warehouse they had taken over and waited; it was nearly one o'clock before the drone of the plane jumped them all into activity. And what with unloading and May tinkering with his motor not heating properly, it was nearly two when they were aloft. The thin fog just hanging there like a suggestion, but when they got up they could see the long grey bank of it moving in from the northwest, the Arctic Ocean.

Erickson wasn't thinking of that however; he sat beside May and looked down in amazement at the wide, almost featureless land-scape.

"Whew," he gasped as the plane dropped, then roared into power again, "it's a bit woozy, but it sure beats snowshoes!"

"When we were trying out those re-arranged orange crates in the Big War," May said, "we always—"

"There!" Erickson interrupted, pointing, "that's the big loop of the Bell River, now, over to the left . . ."

Millen's head came between them from behind, looking along Erickson's finger as May banked left.

". . . it should be straight ahead." Erickson was straining to see over the motor, the blur of propeller, "somewhere straight."

May tilted the plane right while flying straight ahead. "See bet-ter?"

Erickson gasped, but recovered. "It's okay, good . . . I can—there!"

"There!" Millen barked at the same instant.

Below them was a line ploughed straight south through soft snow. May cut the plane down, easily, and they were roaring along very low and close beside the trail.

"Even with those big shoes," Erickson was very excited, "even with them he sinks in a foot, look how deep!"

"Six weeks on the trail," Millen murmured to himself. "Unbelievably strong."

"Oh oh," May said, looking ahead. "See that?"

"Caribou," Erickson exclaimed.

"Yeah, and those tracks . . ." May did not have to continue. In two minutes they had followed the tracks directly into the huge herd like an immense brown and grey blanket rippling over the snow. It was heading west, individual animals stopping to paw through the snow as they moved. The 'lice of the tundra', from above they looked like tiny pointed boats bloated in the middle with their wide thrust of antlers like over-grown brush at the head, and as May came in low over them they scat-tered in terror. They seemed to spray in every direction like wind parting water, lunging through the soft snow, the herd so big that even from the air they could not see the end of it in either direction. Part of it had already rolled down the bank onto the ice of the Bell River and across, west, perhaps moving towards shallower snow along the Porcupine River.

"He uses everything," Millen said to himself in a kind of wonder. "Blizzards, mountains, caribou . . ."

"Who knows where he'll come out," Erickson said. "That herd's so spread out we'll have to—"

"I have to go back," May said, very worried.

Millen's face at his shoulder jerked towards him, but the policeman controlled himself. "You out of gas again?" he asked, ironic.

"No," May did not catch his tone; he was staring at the cloud bank towering above them now out of the west like seething cliffs, "it's that fog, if it—"

"Okay," Millen said, "drop me here on the river."

May stared at him, their noses almost touching. "Are you crazy? If I bust a ski down there, I'm finished."

"I thought you could fly anywhere there's air!"

"Look at that coming in!" May was as furious as Millen. "My wings ice over and we all go down like a rock!"

"Your bloody excuses," Millen said in his ear, quiet as a snake. "Can you make one little circle over the river?"

Albert Johnson crouched under the river bank. His frost-ravaged face looked like a stripped, blackened skull. He held a chunk of caribou calf meat in his bloodied hands and he was chewing on it. He warmed his hands by placing them alternately in the torn-open body of the spring calf beside him while he gnawed at the raw, thick meat, hacking chunks off with his skinning knife close to his teeth and chewing voraciously. He did not stop chewing, or even hesitate as the roar of the plane thundered over him. Only his eyes followed the circle of its sound above him, the terrified snorting of the caribou as they fled before this impossible horror hammering out of the sky. And the clicking of their numberless hooves continued as steadily as ever long after the sound of the plane faded into silence.

Erickson said, "He must be somewhere close around that herd."

He glanced at May, then back to Millen leaning backwards behind him. They both sat like stones. But Erickson had to talk; the plane droned steadily forward into what seemed milky mist featureless as white blindness seeping out of the edgeless sky and the trapper had to talk.

"I'da never believed Bert could do something like this. He was never that strong, no more than usual, he just—"

"You've got to anticipate," May said at the windshield, to the fog settling in drops of instant ice there. "How do you think I've survived this long? If you don't have the brains to anticipate, you don't fly up here. Not more than once."

Millen stared at the ribbed ceiling of the plane. He said nothing.

Far behind and below them, Albert Johnson had threaded his way out of the caribou herd. He was becoming a small misty figure on the frozen river, and he was heading south.

# 12

EAMES' SMALL ARMY had finally arrived at La Pierre House. Exhausted, its dogs worn out from the ferocious wind and fog and deep soft snow in the mountain passes, it took over the Jackson brothers' warehouse and by the swinging light of coal-oil lamp carried in the equipment frozen hard from weeks in double-walled tents and on jarring dog sleds. At last this interminable chase was turning a bit more bearable; a building with solid walls, heatable. Another Mounted Police officer had come in with several trappers from Old Crow, including Johnny Moses, a Dene tracker, and together with the other sleds that dragged over the Richardson Mountain that afternoon, almost thirty men were settling in. Crowded, but warm.

Eames was checking a list in one corner as man after man reported to him. Hersey worked near him on the radio. Riddell and a trapper were fitting battery connections, but Hersey could not seem to concentrate on that; he kept glancing at Millen sitting on a pile of trail gear against the wall. The corporal was still in outdoor clothing, the hood of his parka not even loosened; intense, oblivious.

Sittichinli moved through the crowded room to hunker down beside Millen; who said without looking up,

"Lazarus, I think he has got power, real power. For cliffs, caribou, for two days of fog—how can I catch him?"

After a moment the Dene said, "Use power he hasn't got."

"Like what? He's got so much gun power—what?"

"I don't know. Maybe words."

"Words?"

Sittichinli bent lower. "People say, bushman won't talk. But if you can find him, get him to talk, words, maybe words could hold him."

Eames too was watching Millen as he worked; when Millen suddenly stood up with his rifle in his hand and headed for the door, Eames said immediately, "Spike."

Millen turned. In the yellow light his face was haggard, almost like a gouged skull.

"If I leave now," he said slowly, "I can make the caribou crossing on the Bell River by sun-up."

The radio suddenly snarled, sputtered behind them, but Millen did not turn that way in annoyance, as he once would have. He simply stood expressionlessly, and Eames could not hide the concern on his face at what had happened to his most competent officer, a man once known as the best talker and pie baker and dancer along the two thousand miles of the Mackenzie River. If he had listened to Millen on New Year's Day, at the cabin, when he wanted—there was nothing to be gained thinking that, but seeing the gaunt face, Eames could almost have wept over this terrible pursuit and what it had already done, no matter how it ended, when and if it ever did, God help them.

"It's . . . too late," he said very carefully, thinking his words through before he said them. "Take three men and start tomorrow morning, at five."

Millen considered that. "I want Lazarus, Erickson, and Knut," he said finally. The radio behind them was settling into a steady, efficient hum and men were gathering around to hear what words would suddenly burst from it.

"Okay," Eames agreed instantly. "And Hersey with the radio."

Millen's face jerked up, livid, and Eames said quickly, calmly, "Let me explain. When the rest of us get going, I want to know exactly where you are, not trail you all over the—"

"Send May up for five minutes," Millen's lip curled sarcastically.

"The ice fog," Eames said steadily, refusing to be angered, "can hold on for days. He can't just—"

"That's why one good man with a pack on his back can . . ." but Millen stopped there. He had turned his face away and Eames could not see what, if anything, he was looking at; the Lee-Enfield rifle motionless in his left hand.

"Inspector," Hersey said at his elbow, "Aklavik is coming in loud and clear."

"That'll keep," Eames said. "Are you agreed, Spike?"

"Yeah," Millen said. And walked to the door in his soundless moccasins, opened it, and disappeared into the cold darkness.

Hersey and Eames looked after him, the same worried expression on their faces. Among the men behind them the radio sputtered, "Iron man Johnson . . ." "Crimson battle looms . . ." but they found themselves momentarily together and alone the way two people in a noisy crowd suddenly can be. Eames looked at Hersey, and sighed.

"Frank," he said, "you're an army sharpshooter, right?"

"Canadian champion, sir, three straight years."

Eames said, very slowly, "Johnson's killed one Mountie, and wounded another . . . he's out in the open now . . ."

After a long pause, Hersey asked quietly, "What's the best spot?"

Eames was studying the floor, still thoughtful. "The shoulder . . . smash his right shoulder." He paused, then looked Hersey in the eye. "But more important, don't miss."

"On one knee," Hersey said, "up to three hundred yards I never miss."

# 13

In the cold but humid darkness long before dawn the five men harnessed their three teams while other men loaded and lashed down the sleds. Eames swung his flashlight in signal and Hersey, Erickson, Lang and Sittichinli gathered around him and Millen.

"We change the lead team every twenty minutes," Millen said. "Stay close together."

"Good luck," Eames said. "Frank, every day at nine and five, report."

"Yes sir," Hersey nodded, and then they all scattered.

Gary Snardon came charging through the darkness; certainly not yet dressed for an Arctic morning but pencil and paper already poised.

"Corporal," he called, "Corporal Millen!"

Millen glanced up from tugging at the ropes of his sled. He said nothing.

"Corporal, sir," Snardon began loudly, "you've been after the Mad Trapper since Christmas and now it's the middle of February, you're the only man alive who's actually ever seen Johnson in all that time and . . . well . . ." his set-up words were faltering at Millen's implacable silence. "I mean, you must know Johnson better than anyone . . . I mean, could I have a comment from you, your feelings about this . . . man, some would say madman, I suppose," he laughed a little, stopped short, ". . . you've been after him almost two months now and . . ."

"No."

Snardon stared at him, disconcerted. Millen's face was as expressionless as a rock.

"Will you . . ." Snardon hesitated, then lunged for the inane question, "Will you actually get him?"

"Yes." Millen turned, spoke to his dogs. They leaped forward, disappeared into the mist.

But the weather was not willing to bend right for them yet. As the day brightened a little towards dawn the mist hardened into ice, the clouds to snow, and a frigid wind began worrying them from the north. They were running with the wind down the Bell River, but by noon when they reached what should have been the caribou crossing, the ploughed, scattered tracks of the herd were already drifted in. Millen led on down the river for another hour, adamant that Johnson was sticking to it, but finally the world merged blankly white and impossible. They camped against small brush in one of the interminable loops of the river that even on their map looked exhaustingly long. In such weather they could pass within fifty yards of Johnson and not know it. If they were still on his trail. He could have turned off the river anywhere. And the snow, of course, need not stop Johnson; it certainly was not cold as they knew it.

Towards noon the next day the snow eased out to a low, thick overcast and they could see again, and move. Millen seemed certain Johnson had stayed with the Bell River; the others had nothing better to suggest so they followed it for three hours, watching the banks as it looped its way steadily south and west in its frozen meandering to the Porcupine, and then, suddenly, the peculiar snowshoe tracks were there again. Like ghosts appearing out of the untouched dust of the snow against the northern bank. They stared at them in wonder.

Sittichinli said, "He didn't move while it snowed."

And they all looked at Millen then, apprehensively; he had led them so unerringly through white wilderness to this exact spot where the tracks appeared again. As if he were reading Johnson out of the very air they were breathing together. But he just gestured, come on, and started along the tracks west.

Not very far. The trail divided at the junction where the Eagle River flowed into the Bell from the south. Two tracks in the soft snow, the same snowshoes, going in two different directions again. Sittichinli studied the tracks quickly.

"He's not so good no more," he said. "Weaker."

Millen nodded; the trail that continued west down the Bell River was smudged, awkwardly double. Almost as if the man who made it could not balance well in his own spoor coming back.

Hersey said, "That trick wouldn't fool a kid."

Millen glanced at him swiftly, then along the track leading south in the dusk up the Eagle River. The footprints sank deep, they were short and draggy.

"He's close."

Lang was studying the map. "The Eagle River won't get him to Alaska," he said.

Erickson had never been happy with this pursuit, and now he spoke uneasily. "Maybe he doesn't know that."

Sittichinli was looking about at the gathering darkness. "No good now, to surprise him."

"Yeah," Lang agreed. "We should camp and start with better light."

Hersey looked at Lang's map. "You bet," he said, "this junction's good, right here. Eames can come fast cross-country, avoid all the river loops."

They all looked at Millen. He seemed to be thinking of something else, still pondering the bent tracks made so recently south in the soft snow, made perhaps just at the moment they themselves were rounding the last bend; as if he was thinking of following along them and camping the darkness away with the man who had made them. As if in the strangely warmish air surrounding them now, the many words the man should have spoken but which had never been heard because they had frozen soundlessly into the terrible cold that had hidden him alone until now, his unspoken words would finally, slowly, steadily unthaw and tonight they would hear Johnson speak at last, his personal words tell them how, tell them why, why.

"I radio Eames at five," Hersey said. "He can probably make it here a bit after daylight, they're that close across country."

Millen shuddered a little; his glance came back from wherever he had been and looked at his four companions, almost with a small surprise.

"Okay," he said after a moment. "Let's set up camp."

# 14

Wop May had hooded the Bellanca's nose with a canvas shell in an attempt to protect the engine from the treacherous damp fog; now that it was snowing, the tent kept the snow off too. He had two coal-oil lamps burning inside and three heaters: it was almost comfortable in the mellow, slightly smelly light. He was working, half buried under the motor cowling and Snardon stood behind him inside the skirts of the makeshift tent. He held his black note book up to the light.

". . . the roof of the world," Snardon read with feeling, "the red-handed killer is on the point of being brought to bay by a tireless posse loping on his trail, wearing down Albert Johnson, as the 'Wolf of Rat River'—"

He paused, looked up and commented to the bulge of May's rear end protruding from the motor, "Too much 'Mad Trapper' stuff—'wolf', show a little imagination for *Bulletin* readers, you know."

But there was no indication from May of any interest; perhaps he was not even listening.

Snardon read on, "Johnson, it is claimed, will go out in a blaze of gunfire. Meanwhile, his pursuers press on. Their faces covered with beards, scarred by frostbite. Parkas slept in for more than a month now are black with grease, their Lee-Enfield rifles—"

May pulled back out of the motor with a carburetor in his big greasy hand.

"Only a fool sleeps in his parka," he muttered, picking up a large piece of canvas and spreading it out with one hand on the snow under the motor. "They don't wear nothing in those caribou bags. Nobody ever does."

Snardon hesitated a moment; looked up. But May was staring through a crack in the tent at the falling snow and cursing silently to himself. In the feeble daylight, the tips of the plane's wings were lost in a white streaked glimmer. Snardon flipped a page over, read another section of his story.

"And high overhead, like an eagle waiting to swoop on its prey from some mountain ey—ey-rie," he pronounced with difficulty, then rushed on, "Wop May and his Fokker airplane pierce Arctic fogs and blinding snow to—"

May suddenly jerked, catching on to what he had heard, "I told you," he roared, "this is no goddamn Fokker, it's a Bellanca! B-e-l-l-a-n-c-a! And does it look like I'm 'piercing' anything, huh?"

"You will, Wop, you will," Snardon said quickly.

May turned with a snarl to place the carburetor on the canvas, and then he noticed something that stopped him. An ancient Dene woman, wrapped in caribou hides and a thick wool shawl, stood at the crack in the tent wall. Peering in, and behind her crowded several Dene children, all gathered under the fog and snow-silvered airplane.

Snardon noticed and stared too.

After a moment May said, "Hey, you want to visit . . . come in, come in, take a seat, there's lots of room. Welcome."

And the old woman came inside soundlessly. She looked about, her soft folded face twitching almost as if she were about to laugh but never quite allowing herself that much motion; she stared directly under the cowling of the motor, the tangle of wires and tubes there no stranger to her than a tree blasted into slivers by lightning, and then at May. He grinned suddenly, easy and open, and she nodded her head. The children came around her, their smell of smoke and caribou hide and campfires abruptly like a heavy cloud among the grease and gasoline and kerosene odour, and then she sank down on the snow near the canvas and the children settled around her. May hooked down a lamp, set it on the canvas and began to dismantle the carburetor.

"I can take off in fog easy enough, if it's dry fog," May explained as he worked with wrenches, screwdrivers. "Even snow if it's not too heavy, and a thousand feet up the sun is shining, sure, right now and the clouds all white and level like a goosefeather blanket. I can fly anywhere here because I've got the spots picked on my instruments now and I can find Aklavik or Arctic Red River under the clouds pretty easy and come down through there and not be more than a few miles out, and I know the country. . . ."

He got his screwdriver inside a particularly difficult connection and was prying it open; he did not see the old woman sitting with her eyes closed, concentrating, did not notice her just then beginning to sway a little as he talked, and hum softly to herself, almost in chant.

"I can do all that, if I have to, and I'd try and get through to them even if I iced up bad, but what's the point? It's that Mad Trapper, running away under this damn fog and snow, and Eames after him now with four teams and that poor over-worked Millen half mad himself from chasing that devil all over cr—"

His voice faded; he was finally aware of what was happening across the machinery from him. The old woman in her small circle of children, her chant rising and falling to the easy lift of her voice. It held on a long, singing sound like something dying far away in snow, and stopped; her eyes opened to him. She studied him, her black depthless eyes not dropping before his steady look in the usual way of Dene and whites.

"One more sleep," she said softly, "and he's gone."

May stared; he tilted forward.

"You sure?"

The woman nodded, her delicate, gentle face unreadable as a folded Buddha. May hunched forward, down in front of her: the children stirred uneasily behind her.

"Look," he said, "I have to help them! This fog . . . can't you do something? I have to!"

The old woman said, gently relentless, "One more sleep."

Behind May, Snardon was scribbling furiously in his notebook.

# 15

IN A SMALL SHELTER of tiny Eagle River spruce the police party had built a lean-to frame and covered it with canvas. The large cooking fire reflected into its low opening and in one corner, in the light and heat gathered there, Hersey bundled up his radio. Erickson fed the fire carefully, stick by stick around two large pots set among the coals.

In the darkness under the spruce beyond the firelight the dogs were growling, snarling. Sittichinli and Lang were throwing them their evening fish.

Millen came round the lean-to, his arms filled with spruce branches. He dropped his bundle there, knelt, and began to arrange the branches carefully on the snow. Crossed over each other, back and forth; the size of a man lying down. After a moment Hersey looked up, watched him; and then Erickson also. The policeman was completely intent on what he was doing, the symmetrical, green fronds of each branch laid out and alternated exactly so that their softness and warmth would hold, cradle each sleeper; a strange concentration on comfort when they had for weeks slept anywhere on hard, settled snow. Millen contemplated the boughs for a moment; his face abstracted, almost dreamy, as if he did not quite see what his eyes were open upon. Then he began to spread the next sleeping place. Thick and softly needled, the exact size of a green man laid out on the snow.

Two tight loops of the Eagle River away, Albert Johnson had made his camp beside a stunted spruce. It was up on the river bank, well back and behind the deep spoor of his snowshoes he could no longer hide in the soft snow. Except for the caribou herd and the brief snowfall—and perhaps the fog—the weather in the Yukon had not helped him. There was no glazed surface here worried constantly by wind as there had been on the eastern tundra slopes and plateaus of the Richardson Mountains; there were no brush-filled ravines here either—only the twisting Eagle River now with its occasional bare fringe of spruce—and most deadly of all, only the soft, deep snow that recorded and held every movement like a blotter, that sucked his strength relentlessly. So he had camped up on the open river bank, his tiny fire dug deep down into the snow without any shelter except the snow's rim.

In the tight globe of light enclosed by the snow Johnson had been examining his equipment. He did this every night now, discarding what he could no longer carry and maintaining that which he could not leave. His snowshoes stood erect on his left, his 30–30, which he had inspected first of course, lay on moose hide at his right. The three separate bundles of matches he had laid out in order on the moose hide, together with small leather and paper sacks of salt and pepper and tea and sugar; there were neat coils of babiche, string, moose-hide laces. At the moment he held in his frost-black hands a box of rifle shells; there were thirty-nine, and after looking at the warm copper and lead gleam of their symmetrical row on the moose hide he slid them into a leather sack and dropped their empty box into the fire. He reached for the .22 rifle, but hesitated. There was a stillness in him, a silence untouched even by the gentle snapping of the flames. He reached for another small sack and pulled out a hand mirror. Looked at himself.

A face overgrown with whiskers, sprayed with ice. Otherwise it was chopped out in hollows, as if cold and exhaustion and hunger had been using a blunt axe to hack him down to the bare bones of his skull.

He thrust the mirror away and reached for the .22. He worked its bolt twice, found it satisfactory, and tied the small rifle to the outside of his pack again. Then he picked up the sawed-off shotgun; he broke it, checked the shell in the chamber, and stowed the gun inside the pack. He counted his shells: seven, and placed them in his left hip pocket.

There was a small flurry beside him and he glanced up without concern. A whisky-jack sat in the light on a sprig of spruce beside him, watching in the intense manner of birds. He studied it in turn, without moving; then looked at a tin pail steaming in the fire. He bent forward, fished in it with a stick and drew out a small piece of tanned leather, already cooked limp. He hung it on the rim of the pail and looked up at the bird: it still sat there, bright eye upon him.

He shifted his feet in front of him then and bent forward, untied his right moccasin. Rags and leather were wrapped inside there: he unfolded that to his bare skin. The three smaller toes were hard and black; he ignored them and began to massage the other two slowly, carefully between his hands in the warm glow of the fire, working at the blotches with his blotchy black hands. He found his heel rubbed raw: bad lacing perhaps on his snowshoes and his foot too numb to notice the danger. He studied the exposed flesh a moment, rubbed open, then glanced up at the whisky-jack.

It had hopped a branch closer. It sat there, chirping a little, its body a small twitch of excitement and curiosity.

Johnson laid his blackened foot on a stick near the fire and leaned forward and took the cooled leather off the tin. He cut several bits from it with his skinning knife and with his thumb flicked a bit near the spruce.

The whisky-jack hesitated; then hopped to the snow and gobbled it up. Johnson tossed another bit of leather closer to the fire. The bird hopped a small circle, but approached the leather and with one swift bobbing of its head gulped that down too.

Johnson leaned forward slowly, offered a bit of cooked leather on his black hand; then he dropped it off his finger tip. The bird sat motionless on the snow, its head cocked, its eye reflecting one bright spot of flame. Then it moved, forward, and Johnson's hand moved very fast, the bird was a flurry of feathers and flailing, spastic claws in his disfigured hand. Slowly his hand tightened on that tiny, living warmth; relentlessly.

In the distance, a wolf howled. Johnson lifted his head to listen.

The men pursuing Johnson heard the wolf howl too: it was closer to them, and several of the dogs answered out of the darkness where they were chained. The men were seated on the boughs in the lean-to, the fire a long livid blaze of warmth in front of them. They had eaten well and Lang was pouring tea out of the black pail into mugs while Sittichinli wiped tin plates clean with snow.

"I don't know," Erickson said slowly, staring into the fire, "their farm in Saskatchewan was never any good. A square mile, more rocks even than dandelions . . . Bert and his dad, their overalls always wore through in front, lifting those big rocks." He shook his head. "My poor aunt must be sick about this, just sick."

Hersey was dismantling his rifle, checking every part. "Why haven't they contacted the police?" he asked. "They've sure heard of it, on the radio."

"Not them," Erickson said, "they wouldn't contact anybody, they'll be just so ashamed about their son . . . no . . . not them."

Millen spoke suddenly, "Your aunt ever have a flower garden?"

The men all looked at him; his continued silence on this patrol had pushed them sometimes to talk incessantly to cover their discomfort, their apprehension at this almost mechanical following, this muscle-destroying pursuit of a spoor that seemed to materialize in front of them out of the very snow itself without origin or maker. A man whose face none of them had ever actually seen. Now Millen was offering Erickson the charred corner of a picture and quickly they all crowded closer to look.

"Yeah," said Erickson doubtfully, "she had a little one, sort of against the house, but I don't know about that."

"That's a real fancy garden," Lang muttered.

"It was in his fireplace," Millen said.

Hersey stared, incredulous. "Johnson carried a picture of a flower garden around?"

Millen nodded, put the scrap away in his clothes. He sat staring into the fire as he had all evening.

"Your cousin ever in trouble with the police?" Hersey asked after a few minutes.

"Not that I know," Erickson said.

"He's in so much trouble now," Hersey was rubbing the bolt of his rifle, "he's one of the best known men in the world. That's quite an achievement."

"Sure as hell nobody knows us poor buggers that's chasing him," Lang swallowed his tea.

"They will," Hersey laughed grimly, "if he shoots another one of us."

But Erickson was still thinking about his cousin. "The message he sent me last summer," he said in his soft, quiet voice, "it didn't sound like he wanted to be alone. Not really."

"It's no good, alone here," Sittichinli said.

"Yeah," Hersey agreed quickly. "You're alone in the city, you disappear between people like nothing, but up here every guy sticks out, anywhere he goes, there's nobody else to leave tracks."

"My third winter up here," Lang said slowly, "I was alone. I saw nobody for seven months. Then you find out what you really are."

"Bert's been alone all winter, eh?" Erickson asked.

"Yeah," Lang said. "But it don't matter, you can't just shoot people."

Hersey levered his re-assembled rifle carefully, snick, snick. "And if you do," he said, "you have to pay the consequences."

Sittichinli seemed to be reading the fire. "I like to hunt," he said, "Dahl sheep, caribou, animals like that, but never a man."

"He is a man?" Millen asked, very quietly.

"I think so. Most of the time."

Millen sat on his spruce bed, his tea mug motionless in his hand. The wolf howled, farther away, and the dogs answered again.

Johnson contemplating his fire also heard the dogs, but he did not lift his head to their sound. He had both his feet uncovered to the fire's warmth: his left foot was frozen black as carved marble. He was shaking a tiny tea bag over a steaming tin. But only a few leaves drifted out of it. He held the bag to his nose, sniffed it, then placed it carefully in the fire.

He leaned sideways and picked up the small paper of sugar. He unfolded the paper, poured the last grains into the hot water, and then flipped the sugar paper into the fire also.

He fished with his stick in the other pot, hooked out the limbs and body of the whisky-jack, sprinkled it with the last grains of salt and began to eat. Carefully, savouring each bit of flesh, snapping each bone in turn and sucking it dry. Sometimes his face twitched in a grimace, but he ate doggedly on. And while he did that his hand reached inside his shirt pocket and drew out the worn black and white picture of the woman. He laid it down on his right thigh, face up, but he did not look at it. He finished cracking the last tiny bone and reached for the tin of colourless water; he held that tightly between his blackened hands, leaning towards the fire so that the warmth from the tin in his hands reflected into his gouged face.

He sipped hot water. After some time he put the tin down and reached into his pack and took out a round blue and red box of Dodd's Kidney Pills. He placed that on his left thigh without opening it. Then he picked up the tin and drank slowly again and again.

He set the tin down in its melted circle of snow, picked up the woman's picture and in the same motion placed it in the fire. It flared up brilliant, leaped into scarlet and golden light.

Johnson took up the hot tin again, held it between his hands. He looked steadily and without focus into the fire as the half-smiling face curled brown and vanished completely into flames.

*Part Five*

# Meeting

It was after ten o'clock next morning when the four dog teams and seven men with Eames at their head came cross-country and over the river bank to meet Millen's party working its way steadily along those indelible tracks. They were moving south on the twisting Eagle River, which at that point turned backwards on itself like a reversed S lying on its back, its two tight loops swinging so close together that from the map it was clear the sluggish stream would soon cut through the thirty-foot banks that now contained it at the bends.

"He's sticking to the river though," Lang told Eames, "no matter how it turns."

"That's walking five times as far as he has to," Eames studied the map, worried. "This soft snow."

"Why's he on the Eagle River anyway?" Riddell asked. "It goes more or less south, he's just getting deeper south into the Yukon."

"He's got a plan," Eames said, "he always has."

"I don't know," Erickson said slowly. "He's just about finished, he won't last long."

"There's a real difference in his stride, now." Lang gestured at the short, uneven spaces between tracks.

They all paused then, looked instinctively at Millen. He was hunched down, working the snow out from between the toes of Hersey's lead dog; the dog licked him swiftly, a long red tongue across his hard hands.

"Will May get into the air today, you think?" Hersey asked.

"If that fog lifts an inch, he'll be up," Eames said, looking back to the map. "He's going crazy just tinkering with his plane."

"I'm sure Johnson's trying to get west into Alaska," Lang said.

"Then why didn't he stay on the Bell?" Eames said. "To get there, that's the river he wants."

Lang shrugged, "He doesn't have a map, in fog, . . . maybe he's not thinking so clear anymore."

"But he sticks to this crooked . . ."

"No firewood," Sittichinli said into his pause, "just along the river."

Eames nodded his head slowly, thoughtfully. The Eagle River lay across the plateau of the map like the aimless blue doodle of a child: how could a man on foot on this flatness without a map possibly master that; there was nothing to trust but his eyes, the agony of his aching legs in that featureless sinking snow. The unsteady tracks curved tight around the bend before them: perhaps he was behind a rock, some trees there, waiting or driven to turn around, cornered by his exhaustion or frozen feet, forced and ready to shoot it out. Or give himself up? If he only would. But after seven weeks it was too much to hope.

"Alex," Millen said. He was among the crowd of men suddenly, his finger pointing, "I'll cut across this loop here."

It made some sense; Eames saw that, maybe they should all . . . and then he noted the small creek again that entered the Eagle at the top of the loop, coming in straight from the west. And they were so close now he could not believe Johnson was even that far ahead.

"What if he heads west here?" Eames pointed to the creek.

Millen shrugged. "Then follow him, I'll catch up."

"Well . . ." Eames hesitated, then suddenly agreed. "Okay, Hersey, you cut across here with Spike, the rest of us follow the tracks and the river."

Millen had already slipped on his snowshoes, wheeled, was legging towards the river bank. Before the other drivers had their teams ready he was wedging his way up the rocky incline. Hersey's dogs yelped in furious excitement and surged after him, the sled with the radio almost tipping at their sharp wheel and run.

Meanwhile, at La Pierre House, May with his Lee-Enfield in his hand was clambering into the Bellanca. The plane hummed steadily, happily, in the drifting mist of fog that seemed to be lifting, but so slowly that only someone who really wanted that to happen might have believed it.

Snardon obviously did not. He stood beside the wing, loaded down with three cameras and a notebook, and remonstrated loudly, "It's still foggy, what if it gets worse and—"

May shouted from the plane, "Who said you had to come! Go in, scribble your little stories."

May shoved the rifle alongside his seat and slammed the door. Snardon was already scrambling through the snow, around the front where the wash from the propeller almost knocked him over.

"Wop, wait, wait!"

And he clambered up on the strut. May grinned at him as he fumbled for the door, then turned to the Dene men grouped behind the plane. He waved, they put their backs into pushing, and with a roar the Bellanca's skis broke free and it began to move onto the frozen misty river.

"I came too far," May growled at Snardon panting in the seat beside him, "that old woman . . . they'll need help, I've come too far . . ." He was busy with his controls. Snardon belted himself in, face blanched, breathing so heavily he was fogging the windows.

While Sittichinli led Eames' dog teams north along the wavering tracks on the Eagle River, Millen was plowing west across the narrow neck of land between loops. He ran on snowshoes as easily as if he were in a team race, his muscles so hardened by the trail that they heaved his big body over the snow relentlessly while the dogs pulling the heavy sled leaped and plunged ahead and floundered again and again, trying to keep up. It was clear Millen was making no attempt to lay a drivable trail: he was simply running in giant steps and Hersey bellowed a curse after him, his dogs confused in the sinking snow of the plateau, then snaked his whip over them, roaring them into more violent effort. Not even the shout, the whip cracking like a rifle could slow Millen.

He was forging ahead with awesome strength, running down now through the brush of the next river bank with amazing quietness, faster and faster. As if he were rushing towards a destiny, as if he felt it might evade him if he hesitated, if he so much as paused for one thought about what he was doing.

Hersey's sled hooked a boulder, spilled over and the dogs lunged, snarled, furious at each other and unable to move it dragging on its side. Hersey tried to unhook it, heave it over, sweating in rage and the radio like lead bricks, and then suddenly he stopped. Far north he could hear the other dogs yelping as they ran the long loop of the river, but even when he held his breath he could hear nothing ahead of him. No sound of movement whatever. Abruptly he leaned down, yanked his rifle out of its sheath on the sled.

"Spike!" he called, "Spike!"

Beyond the spindly spruce fringe of the river bank, far ahead of him, he could see and hear nothing; not a sound. Hersey leaped forward, plunged past the dogs still snow tangled in their fight and lumbered after Millen. He had no breath to call, he simply hurled his body forward. He tripped, fell, and struggled erect again, to his feet, gasping, his rifle choked with snow. He had to get to the river!

Millen was already there. He slid out of the river brush, momentarily lost his balance but righted himself while sliding and looked up. At the white blank of the river curving before him.

There was no track there; anywhere.

Millen hesitated, his eyes skimming across the river again and again. The sunlight was brighter here, but there was certainly no track, nothing the whole width of the river and he began to run north on its hard surface. Running a wide curve towards the opposite bank, for if Johnson had suddenly left the ice and turned—he heard a sound and ploughed to a stop.

At the edge of the bank, where the river curved. Sounds of a man, crunching, at the bend of the river, right there—

A man appeared; stopped. Fifty feet away from him. A strangely small man standing on the snow with large snowshoes, an enormous burden on his back. Into the instantaneous freeze of their two bodies came recognition: the sunlight coming streakily through the lifting overcast revealed them to each other. At last.

Albert Johnson and Spike Millen stood face to face again. On the snow of a frozen Yukon river. And this time they both had rifles in their hands so it was more important than ever that they speak, that they say such words to each other as would hold them in their humanity, that would keep those rifles slanted down across their hips, pointed away from each other's poised bodies which, hard muscled and driven to exhaustion as they were, could nevertheless never survive the brutality of exploding lead.

"Spike!" Hersey's faint voice in the brush of the bank. "Spike!"

Johnson deliberately cocked his rifle. Still holding it down, low, and Millen did that too. But then he raised his left hand from it, a warning, a greeting, perhaps, his mouth opening and Lazarus' words gathering there, to say, 'Don't', to ask, 'Why?'

"Bert," Millen said, "easy, easy Bert, Karl's here. He's here, your cousin."

In the sky above them they heard a distant growing roar. Both looked up instinctively. The unmistakable sound of the approaching Bellanca.

A tiny dot coming in fast and low from the northeast.

Eagle River, Yukon. Johnson's body lying on the ice, February 17, 1932

The two men on the river turned their heads to face each other again. Their bodies still anchored in their snowshoes, still frozen in the posture in which they had recognized each other at last, their trail-worn faces rigid, peering forward. Shadow images. But they were too far apart to really see what those opposite eyes could have told them, what the bodies forced for forty-nine days through brush and ravine and river and mountain by those indomitable minds could have explained, because there was Hersey screaming "Spike!" in one snow direction, the

plane coming from the air in the other, the world surrounding them, and there, at the broad invisible bend of the river, the clamour of dogs: Eames and his men rushing relentlessly up the track that led all the way back through the mountains to that canyon on that nameless creek where Paul Thompson had been killed by the rifle Johnson now held in his hands, and there was no way a word, a gesture from Millen though his hand was still up, his mouth still frozen open, would ever stop what was going to happen here. Had to happen.

"Listen, Bert, your cousin Karl, your . . ." Millen said into the air between them; hopelessly. "Bert."

Johnson's rifle swung up and so did Millen's. The shots sounded like one.

Johnson's left hip seemed to explode. He was spun around by the force of it, but he fell on his belly facing Millen, his rifle still up and in his hands.

Millen crashed backwards, flat in the snow.

For a long moment there was no movement on the dead-white river; only the two men down, one sprawled wide on his back, one in tight on his belly. And the sound of the plane droning steadily closer and the men around the bend now screaming at their dogs for speed, the sound of the double shots hammering like warning bells in their heads.

Hersey stumbled out of the brush at the river bank and froze: Millen down, in front of a body with a huge pack on its back. A rifle.

But the pack moved: a head was rising there to the rifle like a point in the snow and Hersey dropped to sharpshooter position. He would have to shoot across Millen . . . his body . . . it was so still on the empty . . . and he brought his snow-slippery rifle in line like target practice and he was clubbed . . . left knee, arm, shoulder, a streak of fire clubbed him as his rifle exploded upwards out of his hands, black crushed him flying backwards.

The Bellanca was coming in at right angles to the north/south loops of the river. Snardon was taking pictures as fast as he could change and reload cameras and May was edging down low, already seeing the long string of dog teams racing around the loop. And then they both saw the black spots of men, probably beyond where the frantic posse could see them, but surely, surely . . .

"There's one . . . two . . ." May muttered, "three!"

"They've got him surrounded!" Snardon bellowed, and grabbed for another camera. "There, in the middle—"

"He's hit two of them," May tipped the plane. "Down baby, down!"

He dived steeply, tilted, shrieking down towards the river in a power dive and the body and broad pack there on the glaring snow, and just as he came down alongside a face and rifle twisted around . . . up . . . and fired. The window beside May's head shattered and Snardon screamed, high, dreadfully.

May swore and swore, fighting the suddenly fluttering lurching plane, the roar of frigid air pounding him from the smashed window. For a moment it seemed they would crash dead into the right bank but the slip of air there lifted them as the motor strained, roaring, and he got it up, up steady into the open air and he could glance at Snardon. Whose mouth was still open in the thin, high scream.

Johnson hunched his shoulders out of his pack and wormed down lower in the snow. There was a kind of cold emptiness at his left hip: he looked there and saw the open crater where Millen's bullet had exploded his shotgun shells. He studied it a moment, then clawed up a mittful of snow and packed it in, quickly, and though the red seeped through it would hold for a little while.

The plane was a distant drone, and Johnson raised his head around the corner of the pack just as the first dog team raced to a stop at the bend of the river. The policeman there wheeling, shouting as more frantic teams rushed up. With painful slowness Johnson reached for the bullets inside his pack.

"Hold the dogs!" Eames yelled, standing on his sled and glaring ahead into the noon brightness of the river curved before him, at the widely scattered blots lying there in the driven snow. Several men ran ahead, grabbing the team leaders. "Okay, now spread out, wide, wide . . . that grey pack, and shoot to kill."

Three men ran left, four right, scattering towards the opposite banks. Eames, flanked by Sittichinli and Erickson, aimed his rifle at the bulge of the pack on the snow and fired. On his left Lang fired too; the pack jumped, but otherwise nothing moved. No rifle, no return shot.

Eames gestured, and the line of men began to move forward, rifles up, deadly alert. Still no movement there, no answering shot.

"Maybe," Erickson said beside Eames, ". . .maybe he's already . . ."

Eames waved to the farthest wing men, near the banks, and they moved ahead so their line now was a curve, a surround aimed towards that one black centre of the pack.

"This time," Eames said to Sittichinli but facing ahead, grim and rigid as a stone, "I'm making sure. Absolutely sure."

He fired again. And all along the line the men began to fire, their shots ripping into the jerking pack; steadily they all advanced.

The pack and the snow were no protection, really. Some of the bullets came in high through the pack, high enough to miss him, and some came in low. In the first fusillade Johnson had been hit four times. But he had gotten his rifle loaded completely again and now the men were close enough and he thrust his rifle around his pack and began to shoot. His face hunched together in pain, shooting steadily. Though the rifle wavered a little in his iron hands.

In the Bellanca that had turned as tight a circle as it could, south of the shooting, May gunned the motor forward.

"If you ain't bleeding," he growled at Snardon, "you ain't hit. A very simple rule."

He thrust the plane down into a long slanted dive. He clasped the controls with his knees, and held it that way with full power on, down, while he hauled out the rifle, cocked it and thrust it through the shriek of cold blasting in at the window.

"Wop . . ." Snardon groaned, "you . . . can't . . ."

"How do you think you make even one kill in a war, you green son of a bitch."

The glazed surface of the snow was rushing at them; May's knees held the plane relentlessly with its dive centred on Johnson. Snardon was bolted rigid in his seat, his mouth a hole of soundless terror.

They could hear the snap of gunfire now. The plane was so low the skis were tickling the snow, a terrible speed and directly ahead of them Johnson's body suddenly heaved up behind his pack as if lifted high by bullets slamming into him from all directions, and then he sprawled as the plane roared past him and May fired, once, and thought he saw Johnson jerk again, face down in the snow, before they were past and he was fighting the plane up over the police to get high enough so the river banks and spruce would not hook him. But he knew now the Bellanca would hold: there was nothing he could not do with this plane and he waggled his wings at Eames as he went up over him like a immense, screaming bullet.

Eames had watched May's approach—if the plane smashed and they had to explain that too—but it roared up from the snow with a salute of wings and he signalled his men. Gradually as the plane's roar quietened upward over the banks, the men stopped shooting. Eames could see the torn pack only fifty feet away; but not anything behind it—except perhaps a sprawled rifle.

Eames moved sideways, staring . . . yes, that was it. The rifle. But then his eyes left that pack and looked directly at what he had seen peripherally all the time he was advancing. He had known what lay there, and he had concentrated himself away from that and now he walked forward, his rifle cocked and a terrible rage boiling in him, if only that criminal would show himself, raise a finger, a hair he would blast him out of existence, it was what he deserved after these days and weeks and months of senseless pursuit and these worse than senseless killings; if he could only do it, now.

But the man did not move. Even when Eames stood with his cocked rifle muzzle three feet from the head he had never seen and could not really see now because its face was ground into the snow, fighting to control his overwhelming urge to shoot, this shape hardly larger than a discarded piece of wood, unmoving.

"Lazarus, go to Spike," he muttered between his teeth.

Sittichinli sprinted forward through the snow, knelt beside Millen. He was dead, his thin frost-marked face up to the sky. In his necessary hunt for Johnson, he too had been hunted; finally.

Sittichinli stood up, shook his head at Eames. And suddenly in that silence of men standing motionless on the white river, a shout.

They looked up: Hersey down in the snow beyond Millen was waving an arm, yelling, "Hey! Hey!" Waving an arm, thank God.

And all the men of the surround exploded into action. Several ran with Riddell to Hersey, others lurched towards Eames and Erickson.

"Lang!" Eames yelled, "Signal the plane to land by Hersey!"

Lang tore off his jacket and waved it at the plane returning low, slowly. Again the wings waggled: May understood. He came down steadily, straight for a landing on the rough river snow.

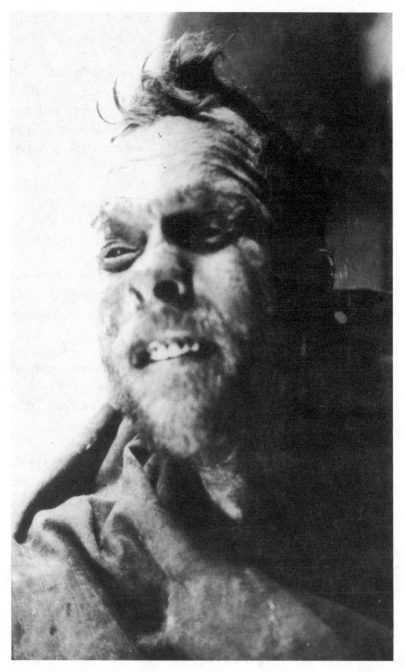

Albert Johnson in death

The men clustered around Millen. Verville wiped his hands across his eyes.

"One bullet," he said after a moment.

Slowly, one by one they turned and walked to Eames bent over the other body. The pack looked as if it had been ripped by rats with long, sharp teeth. The inspector had laid out the guns, found a small box of pills and dropped that, pulled out a tobacco tin with a huge bullet hole torn through the side. He opened it: punctured fifty-and hundred-dollar bills sprawled out. The men stared down, not making a sound.

There was nothing else in the pack: not a scrap of food, not a shred of paper. Eames thrust his hands into pockets, nothing here, there . . . and suddenly he jerked out a paper.

". . . break in and search as necessary," he read slowly. It was Millen's original search warrant; they had the right body all right, the one they had hunted.

Eames looked up at the dark circle of men above him. The sound of the plane died on the river beyond them, and Erickson was looking down steadily at the twisted shape, the face down in the snow. A man's body so incomprehensibly small, how could it have run so long, led them all in this terrible chase . . . its worn clothes now torn by bullets, and never make a single human sound. Nothing; only the crack of a rifle.

Suddenly Sittichinli bent down and in one powerful motion lifted the body up out of the snow. The face turned up.

The men gasped.

Rime, clots of snow ground into whiskers, the cowlick of black hair frozen above half-open eyes showing only white; flared nostrils; the gouged, concrete face wiped clean now of everything but snarl. Frozen snarl and teeth. As if the long-clenched jaws had tightened down beyond some ultimate cog and locked their teeth into their own torn lips in one final wordlessly silent scream.

"That . . ." Erickson murmured, "he's not my cousin."

"What?"

"I never saw him before," Erickson said.

Everyone stared at the trapper, then back down at the twisted, snarled face.

"Then . . . who is he?" Eames said slowly.

Sittichinli holding him said, in wonder, "He's gone away."

Eames was staring at the red crater of the hip. "Well," he said, finally. "We've got him now. We'll know soon enough."

"No," Sittichinli said. "He's gone away. We never know him."

Radio broadcasts around the world announced, again and again, the end of the pursuit and city newspapers everywhere ran dated "Highlights of Manhunt" lists with their front-page stories; the *Edmonton Bulletin* of Thursday, February 18, 1932 finally got the thick red headline it had wanted: RED-HANDED FIEND, RIDDLED WITH LEAD, MEETS END FIGHTING. But the picture the paper ran under that headline, a man in a fur hat standing quietly with his hands crossed behind his back, was not the man who had been shot.

The six-man coroner's jury meeting in Aklavik that same day concluded "the man known as Albert Johnson came to his death from concentrated rifle fire. . . . We are satisfied that the party had no other means of effecting his capture."

The Royal Canadian Mounted Police tried to trace fingerprints they lifted from the frozen corpse, to trace the serial numbers of the various guns and the $2425 in Canadian and American currency, to trace the dental work that Dr. Urquhart itemized in his physical examination report. But when Wop May flew Edgar Millen's body home to Edmonton for burial on February 28, to the skirling of pipes and the respectful attendance of a thousand mourners, nothing further had been discovered. In fact, fifty-six years later, when Lazarus Sittichinli, the last survivor of that extraordinary manhunt, died in Aklavik at the age of ninety-eight, nothing more would be certainly known about "Albert Johnson" than what Eames already knew kneeling in the snow on the Eagle River, surrounded by his quiet men, all of them seeing that tortured face for the first time.

*. . . the silent man*
*having leapt their ring walked back*
*and baited their pride with his spent body*
*brought them the cry they sought and only kept*
*his silence . . .*

–Robert Kroetsch, "The Poem of Albert Johnson"

Edgar Millen Park, Edmonton, dedicated 1968

# Rudy Wiebe Bio

Rudy Wiebe was born on a bush farm in rural Saskatchewan, and moved to Alberta when he was twelve. The son of Russian immigrants, he started to learn English at the age of seven. Today he is considered one of Canada's leading literary icons.

His extensive work, both fiction and non-fiction, centre on the plight of the prairie people, including the Mennonite and Aboriginal peoples. He has been awarded the Governor General's Award twice for his works of fiction: In 1973 for *The Temptations of Big Bear*, and again in 1994 for *A Discovery of Strangers*. He has also won the Royal Society of Canada's Lorne Pierce Award, The Charles Taylor Prize for Literary Non-Fiction in 2007, and was made an Officer of the Order of Canada.

Rudy currently lives in Edmonton, Alberta.